SUBJECT TO FICTION

SUBJECT TO FICTION

Women teachers' life history narratives
and the cultural politics of resistance

PETRA MUNRO

OPEN UNIVERSITY PRESS
Buckingham · Philadelphia

Open University Press
Celtic Court
22 Ballmoor
Buckingham
MK18 1XW

email: enquiries@openup.co.uk
world wide web: http://www.openup.co.uk

and
325 Chestnut Street
Philadelphia, PA 19106, USA

First Published 1998

A catalogue record of this book is available from the British Library

ISBN   0 335 20078 8 (pb)   0 335 20079 6 (hb)

Library of Congress Cataloging-in-Publication Data
Munro, Petra, 1958–
    Subject to fiction : women teacher life history narratives and cultural politics / Petra Munro.
        p.   cm. – (Feminist educational thinking series)
    Includes bibliographical references and index.
    ISBN 0-335-20079-6 (hb). – ISBN 0-335-20078-8 (pb)
    1. Women teachers – United States – Biography.   2. Women teachers – United States – Social conditions – History.   3. Sexism in education – United States – History.   4. Feminist theory – United States – History.   5. Oral history.   I. Title.   II. Series.
    LB2837.M86   1998
371.1'0082–DC21   97-43963
                                                                                                              CIP

Typeset by Type Study, Scarborough
Printed in Great Britain by Biddles Ltd, Guildford and King's Lynn

In memory of my brother
Steven Eric Munro

Contents

Series editors' foreword

At the end of the twentieth century it is not a new idea to have a series on feminist educational thinking – feminist perspectives on educational theory, research, policy and practice have made a notable impact on these fields in the final decades of the century. But theory and practice have evolved, and educational and political contexts have changed. In contemporary educational policy debates, economic efficiency rather than social inequality is a key concern; what happens to boys is drawing more interest than what happens to girls; issues about cultural difference interrupt questions about gender; and new forms of theory challenge older frameworks of analysis. This series represents feminist educational thinking as it takes up these developments now.

Feminist educational thinking views the intersection of education and gender through a variety of lenses: it examines schools and universities as sites for the enacting of gender; it explores the ways in which conceptions of gender shape the provision of state-supported education; it highlights the resistances subordinated groups have developed around ideas of knowledge, power and learning; and it seeks to understand the relationship of education to gendered conceptions of citizenship, the family and the economy. Thus feminist educational thinking is fundamentally political; it fuses theory and practice in seeking to understand contemporary education with the aim of building a more just world for women and men. In so doing, it acknowledges the reality of multiple 'feminisms' and the intertwining of ethnicity, race and gender.

Feminist educational thinking is influenced both by developments in feminist theory more broadly and by the changing global educational landscape. In terms of theory, both poststructuralist and postcolonial theories have profoundly influenced what is conceived of as 'feminist'. As is true elsewhere, current feminist educational thinking takes as central the intersecting forces that shape the educational experiences of women and men. This emphasis on the construction and performances of gender through both discourses and material practices leads to an attitude of openness and questioning of accepted assumptions – including the underlying assumptions of the various strands of feminism.

In terms of the sites in which we work, feminist educational thinking increasingly addresses the impact of 'globalization' – the impact of neo-laissez-faire theories on education. As each of us knows all too well, the schools and universities in which we work have been profoundly affected by the growing dominance of ideas of social efficiency, market choice, and competition. In a rapidly changing world in which an ideology of profit has come to define all relationships, the question of gender is often lost, but in fact it is central to the way power is enacted in education as in society as a whole.

The books in this series thus seek to explore the ways in which theory and practice are interrelated. They introduce a third wave of feminist thinking in education, one that takes account of both global changes to the economy and politics, and changes in theorizing about that world. It is important to emphasize that feminist educational thinking not only shapes how we think about education but what we do *in* education – as teachers, academics, and citizens. Thus books within the series not only address the impact of global, national and local changes of education but what specific space is available for feminists within education to mount a challenge to educational practices which encourage gendered and other forms of discriminatory practice.

Kathleen Weiler
Gaby Weiner
Lyn Yates

Preface

We are delighted to include this book in this series. In her study of the lives of three women teachers over a fifty-year period, Petra Munro engages many of the major issues facing feminist educational theorists today. She uses an analysis of these lives to explore fundamental questions of truth and the making of history. Although she frames this work as a study of three women, Munro's interests range far beyond the specifics of these lives. Her analysis raises questions of representation and the construction of subjectivities with broad implications for feminist scholarship.

Central to this study is a concern with cultural representations of the woman school teacher. But equally central is a focus on the construction of subjectivity more broadly and on the possible meanings of resistance and agency. Acknowledging the importance of unveiling the transparency of authorship, Munro weaves her own intellectual history into a history of various strands of critical social theory that have developed in the years since the 1960s, as educational theorists have moved from a neo-Marxist analysis to one influenced by poststructuralist and postcolonial understandings. As Munro charts her own intellectual journey, she provides guideposts for various readings of these specific lives. In her analysis of the developments within feminist theory more broadly, she also sets out the major shifts that have shaped feminist educational thinking, from a liberal feminism that sought equality for men and women in the existing world without challenging the nature of power relationships, to a structuralist feminism that emphasized the oppressive power of institutions and language to interpellate subjects, to a poststructuralist feminism more concerned with the process of the construction of meaning and subjects – a process seen as constantly shifting and unstable.

In the central chapters, we are introduced to three fascinating women. Through their own narrations, these teachers present their own stories and their own framing of the meaning of their lives. Munro respects these narratives yet manages to follow a difficult course in both validating their presentation of their lives and providing her own commentary and analysis.

Munro's concern in this book is ultimately political – both to respect and give voice to women who otherwise would be forgotten, but also constantly to question her own involvement in the production of this history and to be self-conscious and tentative in her analysis of the stories she has elicited. She is aware of the ways in which we all construct our life narratives within particular moments in time and the way these accounts are inevitably discursive constructions, fictions of a kind. But one of the great strengths of this book is the self-conscious way in which Munro respects the 'subjects' of her research at the same time as she is aware that both their accounts and her own interpretation are in some sense 'fiction'. The questions Munro raises here challenge us as teachers and scholars to reflect on and expand what we understand as 'feminist educational thinking'.

Kathleen Weiler

Acknowledgements

Without the time and commitment of the three women who participated this project could not have been realized. They were generous with their time, patient with my endless questions and enthusiastically supported this work. Sharing their life stories with me was truly a gift of inspiration and hope of what education might be. I am honoured to have shared in the lives of these women, and my greatest thanks goes out to them.

Many people, in numerous ways, have contributed to this work. The research was originally conducted as part of my dissertation research. I am indebted to the Center for the Study of Women in Society at the University of Oregon for their assistance in providing me with the Jane Grant Dissertation Fellowship, which funded the research for this project. My dissertation committee was more than a committee. Their faith in my abilities, trust in my meanderings and complete support made this project possible. I cannot adequately thank Janice Jipson, David Flinders, Harry Wolcott and Barbara Pope for their invaluable and astute guidance throughout a difficult journey.

A very special thanks goes out to my fellow graduate students. The opportunity to share my thoughts and struggles with others engaged in the same process made this a richer work. I particularly thank Tony Catalano, Gretchen Freed-Rowland, Ellen Givens, Robin Heslip, Karen Jones, Kathy Long, Ursi Reynolds, Twila Souers and Susan Victor. Special thanks to Mary Decker for her invaluable help in transcribing all of the interviews, as well as her personal support.

Since leaving the University of Oregon six years ago to take a position at Louisiana State University my network of support has expanded tremendously. I could not have anticipated the rich community of scholars that would become my home. I am indebted to Jon Davies, William Doll, Denise Egea-Kuehne, Mary Ellen Jacobs, Wendy Kohli, Michelle Masse, Elsie Michie, William Pinar, Nancy Spivey, Anne Trousdale and Tony Whitson for their encouragement and ongoing belief in my work. They have challenged my thinking in ways that I hope has made this a more complex work.

I have also been privileged to work with an outstanding group of doctoral students, who continually ask questions that make me realize the taken-for-granted nature of my thinking. They include Natalie Adams, Toby Daspit, Cheryl Edwards, Jeff Gagne, Vikki Hillis, Shelley Kies Wells, Judy Konikoff, Doug McKnight, Marla Morris, Anne Pautz, Molly Quinn, Elaine Riley, Tayari Salaam, Denise Taliafero and Steve Triche.

I am also fortunate to benefit from the friendships with colleagues whose own scholarship has been crucial to mine. In many cases their ground-breaking works have paved the way for this work. I am honoured to include among these friends Margaret Crocco, Elizabeth Ellsworth, Jesse Goodman, Ivor Goodson, Mary Hauser, Nancy Lesko, Andra Makler, Janet Miller, Mimi Orner, Joanne Pagano and Kathleen Weiler. Two colleagues deserve special recognition. Jance Jipson, my (wo)mentor, has provided the guidance that was essential to my becoming a scholar. She taught me how to negotiate the world of academe without losing my soul. For this I am eternally grateful. Wendy Kohli, my colleague, fellow 'good girl', neighbour, yoga buddy, and dear friend, provides daily reminders that I am a strong, powerful woman. I am honoured to call her friend.

A special thanks goes to Leslie Bloom, my colleague, co-researcher, co-author, Mexico-travel companion; the woman who taught me the true art of holidays, and the source of endless hours of discussion regarding narrative, subjectivity and gender. Her intellectual rigour and brutal editing have been central to shaping this work. My current writing group, consisting of Wendy Kohli and Becky Ropers-Huilman, also deserves special thanks for reading endless copies of chapters. Their critical questions and gentle reminders that I had already used 'complex and contradictory' a million times made this a stronger piece. For their ongoing support over the course of the past years I also thank Irene Di Maio, Kate Jensen, Michelle Masse, Anna Nardo and Betsy Wing. Thanks also to Shona Mullen, Anita West, Maureen Cox and Janet Howatson from Open University Press for making this a smooth process.

My friends have been key supporters of this work. By always being willing to listen and confident in the importance of this scholarship they have helped me in more ways than they will know. The years throughout which this book was written were difficult ones at best, but the love and support of the following people sustained me and saw me through those times. I am indebted to Philip Bennett, Patty Lowry, Cassie O'Mara, Charna Rosenholtz and Wayne Selvig for always being there for me.

Finally, thanks to my family, whose constant support over the years and belief in me are at the heart of this study. I found the space and quiet I needed to envisage the original dissertation as a book while spending two summers in Colorado with my sister Tina and her family. My nephew, Eric, provided welcome relief from the computer and brought joy that always rejuvenated me; as a result I am now Disney literate. I lack the words to thank my parents, Gisela and Bill Munro, for all they have done for me. Knowing they are in my life makes all the difference.

In particular, I owe a special debt to my brother, Steven, whose faith in me has meant so much. My only regret is that he is not with us to see the final completion of this project. Even during the height of his illness he took an enthusiastic interest in this work. He read numerous chapters while in bed and always had encouraging words for me. His courage and strength in fighting the battle against AIDS has been a constant reminder of the many struggles to create a more humane society. It is to him that this work is dedicated.

Introduction: impossible fictions

An introduction presumes the existence of a subject, and turns upon that existence necessarily, for in turning to introduce the subject, one expects to find it properly named and placed within an interpretive framework that makes it recognizable, makes it finally symbolically or semantically identical to its name.

Leigh Gilmore 1994:1

I did not want to be a teacher. Teaching was women's work. And yet, the 'subject' of this book is the woman teacher. Who is this subject: the school marm, the spinster, the mother–teacher? These are 'subjects' constructed out of desires and fears that are not my own. They are fictions. Fictions that nevertheless function as truths.[1] Fictions to which women teachers are subject. As Valerie Walkerdine (1990) suggests, being a woman teacher is an impossible fiction. To be a woman is to lack authority, knowledge and power. To be a teacher is to have authority, knowledge and power. Thus to be a woman teacher is to take on what Maxine Greene (1992:17) calls a 'fictitious self'. The three life histories of women teachers re-presented in this book are an attempt to understand how women negotiate a self within and against cultural norms and expectations in which 'women are either absent or represented as the objects of knowledge, rarely its subjects' (Pagano 1990:xvi).

Listening to and interpreting women's lives has been central to the feminist reconstruction of the world (Personal Narratives Group 1989). That 'gender' is crucial to this understanding is the very contribution of feminism. Yet, the notion of woman, positioned within language as a 'subject', is a masculinist construction of an essentialized self, which feminists have sought to disrupt (Butler 1990). If there is no such category as 'woman', since gendered 'identity' is a construction of masculinist binary thought (Cixous 1981; Irigaray 1985), what becomes of the subject, traditionally thought necessary for resistance? Interpreting the narratives of women teachers, I paradoxically seek simultaneously to create and disrupt the notion of the subject. To talk of the 'subject' in these postmodern times seems obtrusively out of style. Like the pair of bell bottom jeans I keep in the back of my wardrobe, these terms seem relegated to the rear, to be stored until they become fashionable again.[2] To revive the subject of woman teacher at a time when subjectivity has become non-unitary, knowledge has become partial, and resistance has become a form of false consciousness, is to enter deeply contested political terrain.

For education feminists, conceptualizing the lives of women educators without reproducing essentialist notions of gendered identity has proved a rich terrain for theorizing the subject (Steedman 1990; Jones 1993; Middleton 1993). One focus of this discussion is the tension between the deconstruction of the unitary, universal subject, which has functioned to highlight gender as a social construction, and the corresponding fear of losing the category of 'woman', central to the political project of feminism. When the subject becomes a fiction, what becomes of the categories 'resistance' and 'agency' thought necessary for social change? Unlike some feminist theorists (Fraser 1989; Hartstock 1990) who fear the demise of the subject as resulting in a lack of political agency, I maintain that an understanding of the subject as non-unitary or fragmented provides new ways to imagine concepts like agency and resistance. This book focuses specifically on how women teachers' construction of subjectivity subverts the fiction of a unitary subject, thus providing a site for reconceiving power, agency and resistance.

I have turned to the life history narratives of three women teachers to understand the politics of identity and the corollary concepts of resistance and subjectivity. The narrative strategies women engage in to create a self (a form of agency) as well as the implications of these strategies for reconceiving curriculum theory are the focus of this book. These strategies are subtle in that they do not embody dominant notions of power, knowledge and subjectivity. They belong to what James Scott (quoted in Paules 1991) refers to as the 'garden' or everyday variety, not only because they are not especially dramatic (like revolution or protest) but because they are 'informal, often covert, and concerned largely with immediate, de facto gains' (Scott 1985:33). In Chapter 1 I reconstruct my evolving theoretical understandings of resistance theory and its corollary concepts of agency, power and subjectivity.

What becomes essential to rethinking agency and resistance from a gendered perspective is a focus on women's discursive practices. My poststructuralist sensibilities remind me that all meanings are culturally and historically contingent; meanings are created by and in social life. We don't create stories; they are fashioned from the discourses available to us. The construction of a gendered subjectivity takes place within and throughout those discourses, which for women teachers are deeply gendered.

Deconstructing the school marm: cultural representations and subjectivity

> Representation of the world like the world itself is the work of men; they describe it from their own point of view, which they confuse with absolute truth.
>
> Simone de Beauvoir (1953)

Women teachers are positioned within and against the seamless narrative of 'women's true profession'. In this story women's motivation to teach is grounded solely in their supposed natural 'maternal nurturance'. Alice Kaplan (1994) suggests that the lesson we learn about teaching is that 'if it is natural' it must be 'too easy to be of much value'. This essentializing discourse obscures women's agency. These scripts define women's role relative to the male plot, in which women's relationship to knowledge is restricted to their naturalized capacity to nurture. Teachers facilitate knowledge but cannot become knowers themselves.[3] Thus, not only are the agency of the teaching act and the meanings women give to their work as teachers obscured, but women's subjectivity and agency are denied.

To represent is to inscribe whose knowledge and what knowledge counts. Representation is a curricular act. Despite the fact that most teachers are women, Mr Chips, the Kindergarten Cop and Sidney Poitier provide the dominant images of teachers. I share Jo Anne Pagano's (1990:xxi) feeling that when I look to these images 'I do not find myself'. After having taught high school social studies for five years I returned to graduate school in the hope that I would come to understand why, in a profession that is predominately made up of women, women's experiences and writings have been excluded from the curricular canon (Hoffman 1981; Grumet 1988). The 'absent presence' (Apple 1983) of gender in research on teaching and of women's voices within a field in which they have been active participants inhibits not only our understanding of the complex lives of women teachers, but also distorts our writing of educational history and curriculum theory (Prentice and Theobold 1991; Munro 1998). Fascinated with questions of who taught and why, historians of teaching have tended to neglect the question of teachers' daily work. In fact, little is known about the daily lives of women teachers and the meanings they give to their work (Tyack 1974). Two factors have contributed to this neglect. First, the gendered construction of teaching as ideologically congruent with women's supposed innate nurturing capacities has obscured the agency of women's lives. Second, the sexual stereotyping and gendered occupational structures resulting from the rhetoric of 'women's true profession' has resulted in representations of women teachers as objects of knowledge, and rarely as subjects (Quantz 1985; Pagano 1990). As I embarked on this research I was initially guided by the question, how do women teachers resist the naming of their experiences by others, which distorts and marginalizes their realities? How do they construct themselves as subjects despite the fictions constructed about women teachers?

Images of schoolteachers include the spinster, the school ma'am, the old maid and the mother–teacher. These stereotypes represent contradictory images. On the one hand, the mother–teacher represents the altruism of women; the self-sacrificing, nurturing woman who complies with her natural duty, in which unconditional love of children signifies the attainment of true womanhood. Adrienne Rich maintains that this fiction of 'motherhood' functions as a form of regulation in which childrearing becomes the individual responsibility of women, and not a societal or communal responsibility. Juxtaposed against this representation of the mother–teacher is the spinster, who is represented as 'embittered, sexless, or homosexual' (Oram 1989). The caricatures of the spinster or lesbian teacher are designed to regulate women's behaviour. The binary images of the mother–teacher and the spinster function to perpetuate the dominant dichotomy of women as good or bad, virgin or vixen, and obscures the complexity, agency and richness of our lives. This dualism is a contradiction that women teachers continually negotiate.

How women teachers 'struggle to write the moving and multiple feminine subjects against the stereotyped woman' (Wexler 1987:96) thus attunes us not only to the sites of conflicting gender norms inscribed in teaching, but to how these stereotypes function as a form of gender regulation. Stereotypes, as Patricia Hill Collins (1990:68) suggests, are designed to make sexism 'appear to be natural, normal and an inevitable part of everyday life' and make the patriarchal control of the profession normative (Apple 1985). Yet women teachers have not simply been acted upon but have negotiated, resisted and created meanings of their own (Hoffman 1981; Kaufman 1984; Casey 1993).

Because of its gendered construction, the teaching profession provides an excellent opportunity to explore the process of how gender ideologies become 'natural' as well as how gendered norms are contested in the daily lives of women teachers. Specifically, how do women's desires and sense of self assume meaning within historically specific discourses and gender ideologies of teaching embedded in notions such as 'women's true profession', 'feminization of teaching' and the 'professionalization' of teaching.[4] It is essential to recognize that these discourses do not represent gender, but are central to the production of gender. In other words, as Denise Riley (1989) maintains, 'women' is not as stable, as inevitable, a category as it seems. My concern is to shift the terrain from asking 'who is the subject?' to revealing how individuals are continually being constituted through discourses as apparently unified subjects. The life history narratives presented in this book suggest that women are not determined solely by these discourses but are active agents in negotiating them. This negotiation of the gendered norms embedded in dominant discourses suggests that the subject is always in production. The site of this ongoing production is the focus of my narrative analysis. I now describe the life history process in which I engaged. Both the possibilities of life history, as well as the problematics, will be discussed.

Narrative as social action: life history narrative and subjectivity

Writing women's lives is, as Helene Cixous (1976) reminds us, no easy task. How can we write as women when the 'woman' subject is a construction of masculinist language, or, in other words, a fiction? The narrative genres available to us – biography, autobiography and life history – are also culturally determined, and thus inevitably gendered as well as raced and classed (Rosenwald and Ochenberg 1992).[5] Feminists have highlighted how these genres assume the male life cycle and experiences as the exemplar for 'writing a life' (Bell and Yalom 1990). These modes of representation authorize stories that are public, individual and linear. Leigh Gilmore (1994:2) maintains that women's modes of self-representation cannot be recognized when they are 'written against the dominant representations of identity and authority as masculine'.

To conduct life histories of women teachers is to take seriously the lives of women teachers. To take seriously their stories was to acknowledge their conversation as more than just 'idle talk' or mere gossip. The three life histories of women educators presented in this book narrate what Alice Walker calls 'mystories'; stories of the way women know themselves. As Carol Christ (1986:16) reminds us, 'the simple act of telling a woman's story from a woman's point of view is a revolutionary act'. In 'naming the gap between men's stories about women and women's own perception of self and world' (Christ 1986:23) women's narratives become a generative space for understanding not only the complexity of women's lives but how women construct a gendered self through narrative. This means including aspects of life stories that have traditionally been dismissed: how women's private and public lives intersect; the impact of the mother–daughter relationship; and the familial and female friendship support networks that sustained women's public activities (Alpern et al. 1992). And, of course, their discourse; how they talk about their lives.

The manner of the telling, the authoring of oneself through story, provides a space for understanding what Bakhtin (1981) calls the dialogic self, the relationship between self and culture. In situating women teachers as 'authors' (Casey 1993), their narratives can suggest the meanings they give to their lives. How individuals construct their stories, the tensions, the contradictions and the fictions, signifies the very power relations and discursive practices against which we write our lives.[6] Thus, the use of language – the myths, metaphors and imagination – in the way that individuals construct a self is a political act (Personal Narratives Group 1989; Portelli 1993).

The current narrative or interpretive turn in the social sciences challenges traditional epistemological paradigms by problematizing the very nature of knowledge as objective and corresponding to any reality of the past (Polkinghorne 1988; Young 1990). This work has been pivotal to the critique of unitary ways of knowing and has blurred traditional boundaries between fact and value, history and fiction and knower and known. By highlighting the storied nature of knowledge, narrative has been critical in problematizing modern forms of knowledge that seem natural but, in fact, are contingent on sociohistorical constructs of power.

My interest in narrative as the primary way in which we organize experience is in its intersection with life history. Life history interviews are themselves texts designed to not only give shape to some feature of experience but ultimately to create a self. As Bakhtin (1981) suggests, there is an intimate connection between the project of language and the project of selfhood; they both exist in order to mean. There is no identity outside narrative. Events or selves, in order to exist, must be encoded as story elements. Narrative, as Ricoeur (1974) reminds us, imposes on the events of the past a form that in themselves they do not really have. Because these are reconstructions, original purity of experience can never be achieved.[7]

Educators have turned to narrative to interrogate the nature of the dominant curricular stories we tell and how these shape our understandings of self (Britzman 1991; Witherell and Noddings 1991; Gough 1994; Pinar 1994; Weiler 1994; Bloom in press) as well as how teacher and student stories and lore (Connelly and Clandinin 1990; Gitlin 1990; Schubert and Ayers 1992; Goodson 1992; Casey 1993; Sparkes 1994) can reshape our understanding of the lived experience of schools and teaching. As researchers we seem to be currently engaged in a romance with narrative. Stories soothe us in troubled times, which seem to require a return to simplicity. But stories are no longer simply stories. The current 'crisis of representation' reminds us that all stories are partial, the teller always 'in flux', and that the tales we tell are never mere descriptions (Clifford and Marcus 1986; Lather 1991; Denzin and Lincoln 1994). Consequently, my own romance with narrative is an uneasy one.

Invisible mending: the search for a method

As a feminist, my original concern in seeking a method was to find one that would allow me to recover the marginalized voices of women teachers and the meanings they give to their experiences. Jane Marcus (1984) refers to this process of recovering women's voices as 'invisible mending'. Listening to women's voices, studying women's writing and learning from women's experiences have been crucial to the feminist reconstruction of our understanding of the world (Personal Narratives Group 1989). The focus on the personal not only allows women to describe, in their own words, their experiences, but also illuminates the contextual, subjective and relational processes from which our understanding of the world emerges.

As I pursued my search for a method, I was initially attracted to ethnography. There is no simple definition of ethnography. William Ayers (1989: 11) suggests that, 'Ethnography is as dynamic and complex as the human beings it undertakes to study'. At the heart of ethnography is cultural interpretation. I avoid the term cultural description since it suggests a false sense of neutrality. In *Writing Culture*, James Clifford (1986:11) suggests that 'the predicament of ethnography is the fact that it is caught up in cultural interpretation, not cultural representation'. In *The Interpretation of Cultures*, Clifford Geertz (1973:15) maintains that 'anthropological writings are themselves interpretations and second and third order ones to boot. They are thus fictions: Fictions, in the sense that they are "something made", "something fashioned"'.

Culture is therefore not 'visible' (Van Maanen 1988:3) in any physical sense, but is the ethnographer's understanding of how people make sense of their world. It is an attempt to interpret the values and belief systems people attribute to their roles and actions. In essence, as Geertz (1973) suggests, ethnography requires conveying the insider's sense-making view. The appeal of ethnography is its acknowledgement of the individual's ability to create, struggle against and negotiate social meanings. Clifford and Marcus (1986:15) suggest that 'culture is always relational, an inscription of communicative processes that exist historically between subjects in relation to power'. Despite the admission that ethnography, and, in fact, all research, is by nature an intersubjective process (Powdermaker 1966; Crapanzano 1980; Langness and Frank 1981; Wolcott 1990) from which one cannot separate one's own beliefs, I was unsettled by the absence of the ethnographer's voice and an account of the process in many ethnographic texts. Feminist ethnographers, including Stacey (1988), Mascia-Lees *et al.* (1989) and Roman (1989), have been critical of ethnographers who present dematerialized accounts of their work. Although the need for self-reflexivity among critical or new ethnographers (Ruby 1982; Clifford and Marcus 1986; Marcus and Fischer 1986) seems to be established, Gary Anderson (1989:255), in reviewing recent trends in ethnography concludes that 'little progress has been made in exploring methods that promote the kind of reflexivity required of the critical ethnographer'.

Despite the multiple attractions of ethnography, both theoretically and practically, I had several reservations about engaging in a full ethnographic study. My explicitly feminist viewpoint, with its focus on transformation, seemed at odds with ethnography's focus on description. This raises a second area of reservation; that of the relationship between theory and research in ethnographic studies. As I understood it, ethnography allows the theoretical constructs to emerge from the field. This assumes that as researchers we can step outside our own theoretical biases. My strong identification as a critical feminist made it difficult for me to enter the field without a preconceived framework for interpretation.

As I was attempting to resolve this dilemma, I was drawn to life history and narrative inquiry because of its potential to highlight gendered constructions of power, resistance and agency (Haug 1987; Personal Narratives Group 1989; Goodson 1992; McLaughlin and Tierney 1993; Smith 1993a). As I read life histories of women (Cantarow 1980; Heilbrun 1988; Aptheker 1989; Bateson 1989), the very personal voices of women, the descriptions of their daily lifes, moved me in profound ways. I recognized that my frustration with classic accounts of teachers' lives like Dan Lortie's (1975) *School Teacher*, Philip Jackson's (1968) *Life in Classrooms*, and Larry Cuban's (1984) *How Teachers Taught*, was not only that they were gender neutral but that they did not have the voices of actual teachers.

I now looked for life histories of women teachers. It was not surprising that I did not find a large representation of women teachers' voices. Among the few are works like *Teacher* by Sylvia Ashton-Warner (1963), although this is an autobiographical life history, *Women's True Profession* by Nancy Hoffman (1981), which presents historical narratives of women's voices through diaries, letters and other written documentation and *The School Ma'am* by Frances Donovan (1938), which presents a composite life history with quotations of interviews with women teachers.[8]

My search then took me to the curriculum literature. Since my interest was in how the curriculum of women teachers reflects resistance to patriarchal norms, I hoped to find the voices of women teachers within this literature. I found a large body of literature on life history and biography, but few of these works focused on presenting women teachers' experiences. The use of life history within curriculum in teacher education has been a means of encouraging preservice teachers to reflect on their lives and educational experiences for the purposes of making explicit their taken-for-granted assumptions about education (Pinar and Grumet 1976; Bullough 1990; Knowles and Ems 1990).

A second use of life history is in understanding the curriculum decision of teachers (Sikes *et al.* 1985; Connelly and Clandinin 1988; Goodson 1988; Schubert 1991). These researchers share a common belief that curriculum is a reflection of the personal knowledge and experience of teachers. Consequently, life history provides one method for examining the process of curriculum. My discovery of the use of life history in this context provided a grounding for my work in exploring the relationship between women's lives and curriculum, and the impact of and their relationships with patriarchal norms.

I sensed that life history was 'the' method I had been searching for, and I now turned to explore the methodological literature, in order to answer the question, 'what exactly is a life history?' Although use of life history flourished among sociologists at the University of Chicago during the 1920s and 1930s, it suffered a decline with the emergence of new research methods that stressed positivistic theory. The current focus on acknowledging the subjective, multiple and partial nature of human experience has resulted in a revival of life history methodology. What were previously criticisms of life history, its lack of representativeness and its subjective nature, are now its greatest strength (Plummer 1983; Geiger 1986). Life history's primary goal is an account of one person's life in their own words, elicited or prompted by another person (Langness and Frank 1981; Plummer 1983; Watson and Watson-Franke 1985). Life history studies provide an opportunity to explore not only the effects of social structures on people but to portray the ways in which people themselves create culture (Dollard 1935; Mandelbaum 1973; Sheridan and Salaff 1984).

Denzin (1970) suggests that the chief feature of the life history is the prolonged interview, which, in fact, consists of a series of interviews in which the participant and the interviewer interact to probe and reflect on the participants' statements. The interview is supported, where possible, by documentary evidence and reports. The advantages of the life history approach for this study are:

- the holistic nature of life history allows for a complete biographical picture
- a life history provides a historical, contextual dimension
- in studying a life history, the dialectical relationship between the self and society can be explored.

For feminists seeking to recover the lost voices of women who have been denied public space because of 'patriarchal notions of women's inherent nature and consequent social role', life history has provided one suitable alternative (S. Smith 1987:7). The greatest strength of life history is in its penetration of the subjective reality of the individual; it allows the subject to speak for himself or herself.

In addition to life history's usefulness for studying persons whose history has been marginalized, life histories are particularly well suited to illustrating some aspects of culture not usually portrayed by other means, such as women's view of their culture (Langness and Frank 1981). According to the Personal Narratives Group (1989), life histories are especially suitable for illuminating several aspects of gender relations including:

- the construction of the gendered self-identity
- the relationship between the individual and society in the creation and perpetuation of gender norms, and
- the dynamics of power relations between men and women.

Life history method can also provide a research methodology that addresses feminist concerns that research be situated contextually, challenges the norm of objectivity by acknowledging the intersubjective process of meaning making and be collaborative and reciprocal. Lastly, by providing opportunities that allow people to become 'visible and to enhance reflexive consciousness' (Myerhoff 1982:101) the life history process can address feminist concerns that research be empowering and transformative. My hope was that life history's potential for illuminating the dynamic interaction between human agency and hegemonic forces would highlight the experiences of women teachers as they negotiated and resisted imposed meanings.

Entering the field

This book has emerged from a larger study in which six life histories were conducted over a six-month period beginning in January 1991. Although my original intention was to collect the life histories of retired secondary social studies teachers, circumstances emerged otherwise. My criteria were based on two assumptions. First, I was eager to collect stories about women teachers who had taught in the 1930s, 1940s and 1950s since little historical information is available for these time periods. In retrospect, I also realize that I feared working with contempories, or those in a similar age group, because it would be too difficult for me to make the familiar strange. Second, I chose social studies teachers because of my experience as a social studies teacher. I hoped this would provide a common understanding on at least one level.

The selection of the 'life historians' – a term suggested by Marjorie Mbilinyi (1989) as an alternative to the objectifying labels of 'informant' and 'subject' – was arbitrary and serendipitous.[9] As I began conceptualizing the project in the autumn of 1990 and contacted friends, colleagues and professional organizations in order to elicit names of potential life historians I was overwhelmed by the response. I knew none of the women prior to our research. All were names given to me by word of mouth. Cleo and Bonnie, after a single phone call to each, agreed to participate in the study. Bonnie, the only life historian who was not retired, provided the opportunity to observe a teacher in the classroom. Both Cleo and Bonnie were in close enough proximity that we could meet on a regular basis. I received Agnes's name from a family friend. Because she lived in a nursing home in Chicago I spent several days with her in the spring of 1991 and then was able to interview her three more times before her death in 1996.

Interviews were the primary source of data. The in-depth life histories conducted with Cleo and Bonnie consisted of multiple interviews, at least five being taped with each woman, as well as several less formal conversations. The interviews were generally nondirected and took place in the homes of the women. I began the first interview with, 'Tell me your life story'. Although the interviews that followed were more focused on particular events, their nondirected nature was maintained. My primary goal was to keep the interviews as open-ended as possible in order to allow the experiences the life historians deemed to be most central to their lives to emerge. All interviews were tape-recorded and transcribed.

At my initial meeting with the life historians I explained the nature of the project and my hope that we would work in collaboration. By being honest about my expectations and eliciting theirs, I hoped the life historians would be full participants in the research process. In addition to stating my research aims, I explained that they would receive copies of all transcribed interviews and that the final narratives would be given to them for feedback. Each participant was also asked to sign the Protection of Human Subjects consent form.

In order to establish as broad a context as possible for understanding the life histories, supplementary interviews were conducted with colleagues, administrators and students. With Bonnie, I was also able to observe her in her school setting for three whole days. This included not only observations in the classroom but of staff development meetings, textbook adoption meetings and a meeting of the Oregon Council of Social Studies. With Cleo, I had the opportunity to meet with her women's group.

Several other ethnographic techniques were employed in this study, including the collection and analysis of personal and school documents. These ranged from teaching materials, articles written by the life historians, curriculum materials, photographs, journals, school documents, favourite books and newspaper articles. In order to obtain specific information regarding the life historians' work and family history, each was asked to fill out a questionnaire. Initially, I asked Bonnie and Cleo to keep a journal of their experiences. I hoped this would allow me to enhance my understanding of the intersubjective process of meaning making. However, they declined to keep a journal (see Epilogue for a further discussion of this).

Since this study is concerned with placing the lives of women teachers within a broader historical context, historical data regarding the communities and the time period in which they taught was also collected. Although I am not an educational historian an attempt was made to understand both the local history and broader historical context in which these women lived.

The last source of data was my own field notebook in which field notes and reflections were documented. As Watson and Watson-Franke (1985:16) point out, due to the intensely subjective nature of the life history it is important to identify the specific and immediate conditions under which a life history is written and related. My personal reflections on the process of conducting collaborative life histories are presented in the Epilogue.

As I reflect on the process of conducting this research, I realize that the selection of the 'life historians' working with me was as much accidental at the time as it now seems logical. I could not have anticipated the connections that linked our lives; the struggles across time and place that served as bridges as well as boundaries. I also could not have anticipated the complex relational dimensions of the research process. My relationships in the field not only provided my primary source of data, but these relationships became the epistemological base from which my interpretations and knowledge claims originated. In constructing the stories of Agnes, Cleo and Bonnie I incorporate my own story throughout as a means of acknowledging the intersubjective nature of knowledge. I weave my own story of the research process throughout the life histories as a way to create a 'tapestry' (Aptheker 1989) of our lives, an interweaving of connections, which is not only central to women's survival, but an epistemological act.

Cautions about life history

As mentioned earlier, my embrace of narrative is also an uneasy one. I engage in life history research with suspicion. As a feminist, this method has been attractive because it provides a method that seeks to 'recover' the voices of women who have traditionally been marginalized. Yet, the very agency of the individual seems undermined by talk of 'giving voice' by reproducing the very unequal power relations that I, as a feminist, seek to disrupt (Munro 1993). In fact, the notion of 'giving voice' has been particularly unsettling because it actually underscores my perceptions of those I was researching as disempowered and conflicted with my understanding of them as meaning makers.[10] What I want to suggest is that there is nothing inherently liberatory about life history research (Goodson 1995).

My second concern is with the potential of narrative research to romanticize the individual and thus reify notions of a unitary subject/hero. The focus on 'teacher voice' and 'teacher stories' arising out of the phenomonological/interpretive tradition retains enlightenment notions of an essentialized self capable of discerning the meaning of experience. The current focus of narrative on recuperating forgotten 'stories' suggests that we can capture experience, thus reifying notions of subjectivity as unitary, essential and universal. This focus on life story as individual stories has been criticized as a form of narcissism or 'navel gazing'. This reconstituted focus on the individual thus potentially functions to deflect the complexities of social life in which racism, sexism and other forms of oppression continue to exist.

Lastly, my uneasiness with life history research is with the potential colonizing effects. Despite the focus on the liberatory aspects of narrative, I know that all knowledge is dangerous. For instance, using such tropes as 'raw materials' (Lincoln 1994) to describe the narratives of the silenced, or to speak of 'exploring' (Goodson and Cole 1994) the teacher's professional knowledge, or constituting subjectivity as 'border disputes' (McLaren 1994) reinvents a colonial relationship. All research is implicated in power relations, and life history research is no exception. These cautionary tales are intended to keep us suspicious of all claims of privilege. What they suggest is the complex ways in which narrative both contests and reproduces positivistic notions of power, knowledge and subjectivity despite claims to the contrary.[11]

In collecting the life histories of women teachers I find myself situated in a paradoxical position. I know that I cannot 'collect' a life. Narrative does not provide a better way to locate truth, but in fact reminds us that all good stories are predicated on the quality of the fiction. We live many lives. Consequently, the life histories in this book do not present neat, chronological accounts of women's lives. This would be an act of betrayal, a distortion, a continued form of 'fitting' women's lives into the fictions, categories and cultural norms of patriarchy. Instead, my understanding of a life history suggests that we need to attend to the silences as well as what is said, that we need to attend to how the story is told as well as what is told or not told, and to attend to the tensions and contradictions rather than to succumb to the temptations to gloss over these in our desire for 'the' story.

Multiple lives, multiple stories

Despite my caution I remain committed to the potential of life history research to enlarge my understanding of the complex ways in which we make meaning. The heart of this book is the three narratives that I have constructed. Born in 1897, Agnes Adams (Chapter 2) was raised on the Kansas Prairie, began teaching at 18 years old in a one-room school, graduated in 1924 with a degree in Early Childhood Education from the University of Chicago, where she studied with Dr Alice Temple (a student of Dewey's), and then spent the next 48 years teaching at the National College of Education, where, upon her retirement at 68 years old, she married for the first time. Despite my original construction of an apparently seamless heroine's story, Agnes's narrative provided profound ruptures that produced a window to the complex and contradictory gender and curricular ideologies that shaped her life. Specifically, Agnes's story prompted me to reconsider the place of female progressive teachers and their connection to earlier generations of reform minded women.

Agnes's decision to enter teaching coincided with what Lynn Gordon (1990) described as a period (1890–1920) of female separatism, social activism and belief in a special mission for educated women. At the same time, educational historians (Ravitch 1974; Tyack 1974; Urban 1982; Kliebard 1986) have described this period as one of centralization and bureaucratization, which occurred as schools adopted a theory of scientific, meritocratic management that emphasized increased efficiency, standardization and reliance on experts (read males). Central to Agnes's story is her negotiation of these conflicting discourses, which signalled on the one hand a special mission for educated women, and on the other hand the deskilling of teachers through increased control of education by experts, which situated teachers as tangential to the curricular process.

For Agnes, women's special mission took its roots in the Kindergarten movement. By no means a coherent unified movement, the diverse and conflicting philosophies of its main advocates (Susan Blow, Elizabeth Harrison, Patty Smith Hill and Alice Temple) provide a unique opportunity to explore the diverse ways in which gender relations were being actively defined by women through institutions like motherhood, childhood and education despite the monolithic views often perpetuated through discourses of 'teaching as mothering' and 'child centered teaching', which represent the work of women teachers as following their natural instincts, thereby obscuring the intellectual and socially tranformative aspects of the work of teachers. Agnes's story highlights the negotiation of the complex and conflicting ideologies that span educational discourse such as progressivism, professionalism and technical rationalism, and gender ideologies such as 'separate spheres', the 'new woman' and 'equality'.

Cleo's story (Chapter 3) echoed my own ambivalence about teaching. Born in the South in the 1920s, Cleo's desire to resist the patriarchal script for women was narrated in her tales of travel, adventure and pursuing academic interests in history and economics in which she was always 'one of the boys'. The tension between her understandings of herself as intellectual (male) and her choice to become a teacher (female) embodies itself in the metaphor of the 'drifter', in which Cleo's continual transversing of gender boundaries disrupts fixed notions of gender identity. Her narrative suggests the need to attend to the complex intersections of gender, class, race, history and sense of place as a way to disrupt essentializing and reductionist understandings of taking up teaching.

Beginning her career in the 1950s as a secondary social studies teacher in the Pacific Northwest, becoming social studies department chair and eventually a district administrator engaged in social studies curricular change, Cleo's narrative initially intrigued me due to the agency with which she rewrote the traditional story of women teachers in the 1950s and 1960s as having 'flat career lines' and 'lacking commitment' (Jackson 1968; Lortie 1975). My desire to interpret her life as 'resistance' was continually disrupted by her claims that she 'could have lived another life and been just as happy' and that she never wanted to be a 'top Joe'. How Cleo writes her life against the imposition of masculine models of work provides a window for examining how subjectivity is constructed. These tensions highlight the conflicts women face on taking up administrative positions in a culture in which power and authority are defined in patriarchal and masculinist terms.

For Cleo, her commitment to bringing about curricular change is not only written against the gendered discourses of 'administration' but within the context of dominant curricular ideologies of the 1950s and 1960s such as the 'Tyler rationale'. Located specifically within her work in the 'new social studies' movement, which re-envisioned social education as student-centred and inquiry based, Cleo's understandings of curricular change are embedded in her understandings of change as dispersal of power, rather than consolidation, as a means of establishing the communities necessary to developing the collective investment in social change. How women teachers experience the process of change is central to understanding the conditions and culture of their work, as well as reconsidering traditional concepts of agency, change and power as a means of problematizing historical narratives of educational reform. Cleo's early retirement in the 1980s, due in part to her resistance to educational reforms prompted by reports like *Nation at Risk* (National

Commission of Excellence in Education 1983), allow us to gain an understanding of current reforms from a life history perspective.

Born in Canada in 1945, Bonnie (Chapter 4) began her teaching career in
the early 1970s and continues to teach secondary social studies in the Pacific
Northwest. Her early experiences working in Volunteers in Service to America (VISTA), the civil rights movement, and union activity have been crucial
to her understanding of herself as a teacher. Her experiences as a social
studies teacher in a middle-class suburban high school, as representative to
the teachers association, and, currently, her role as social studies department
chair have continued to shape her understanding of herself as teacher–advocate and activist.

Bonnie's narrative reveals the tensions between her understanding of herself as a 'do-gooder' and the context of education, which historically has
denied the agency of women teachers (Quantz 1985). Bonnie's investment in
the discourse of teacher as activist, although reifying a masculinist plot, conflicts with the competing discourse of 'professionalism', dominant in the
1980s, in which agency and autonomy are sacrificed for the greater good.
Thus, the discourse of professionalism works in conflicting ways to reify traditional female norms of sacrifice and selflessness while simultaneously
inscribing masculinist notions of work. Bonnie's experience of this imposition was narrated through her experiences of the regulation of her body.
Drawing on Foucault's genealogy of discipline and punishment as well as
Sandra Bartky's and Judith Butler's work on the body as a site of regulation,
I interrogate the gendered norms embedded in notions of professionalism.

Through listening to their stories, I began to identify my own. Perhaps,
more importantly, I connected with other women teachers and our stories
intertwined to create a history, a context for teaching and a sense of community that I had been denied. Like Andra Makler (1991:32), the process of
collecting life histories of women teachers 'reestablish[ed] the threads of
continuity between us' and as a result I 'gain[ed] a different perspective on
my life in relation to the lives of women who preceded me in time, women
to whom I see myself linked by gender and circumstance, quite apart from
my will to have it so'.

If women teachers are 'subject to fiction', I simultaneously acknowledge
that my search for the 'real' woman teacher is also a fiction. Instead, it was
the ongoing and continual process of constructing a self that was a primary
form of agency. In Chapter 5 I present an analysis of the narrative strategies
engaged by the life historians and the implications of these for rethinking
notions of power, agency and subjectivity. I explore how the narrative strategies used in these women's telling of their lives suggests ways to reconceptualize resistance as grounded in the daily relational activities of teacher's work.

Finally, I conclude this work with an epilogue in which I deconstruct the
process of conducting life history research. My original assumptions regarding the collaborative and egalitarian nature of the life history process are

re-examined in light of my actual experiences. Most importantly, it seemed that 'getting it right' had less to do with adhering to life history method and everything to do with acknowledging the relational and political dimensions of the research process.

Notes

1 As Walkerdine (1990) points out, gender ideologies, although fictions, function as a 'truth-effect', thus making natural what is a social construction.

2 Shortly after I wrote this I read McWilliams's *In Broken Images*. She goes so far as to suggest that the postmodern trend has relegated writing about oppression, agency and social justice to the ranks of the 'neanderthal' (McWilliams 1994:2). Her discussion of 'PMT' (post modernist tension) highlights the conflicts for feminists who embrace certain aspects of postmodernism while not wanting to give up the political work of social change.

3 Martusewicz (1992) discusses the relationship between power and knowledge in relation to women teachers.

4 Clifford (1989) contends that gender ideologies, like the concept of domesticity, have been used in contradictory ways to argue the merits of male versus female teachers. During periods of economic decline, as in the 1930s, gender ideologies suggesting that a woman's place was in the home were promoted through publications of reports like *Teaching as a Man's Job* (Phi Delta Kappan 1937).

5 For a further discussion of the feminist and postmodernist critiques of auto-biography see Heilbrun (1988), Miller (1991) and Gilmore (1994).

6 The intersection between narrative and education is articulated by Witherell and Noddings (1991), who suggest that narrative can elucidate the construction, transmission and transformation of culture. Goodson (1992) also suggests that narrative offers a substantial step forward in the representation of lived experience in schools.

7 However, although experience can never be achieved, I am reluctant to give up a material world. As Freeman (1993) suggests, furniture only exists through language but that doesn't keep him from bumping up against it.

8 At the time that I conducted this search the life history research of Casey (1993), Etter-Lewis (1993), Middleton (1993) and Weiler (in press) was not yet available.

9 The term 'life historians' is suggested by Mbilinyi (1989) as an alternative to the objectifying labels of 'informant' and 'subject'.

10 LeCompte (1994:10) suggest that life histories concern with 'giving voice' as a means of adding 'counter-hegemonic stories' is embedded in a narrative structure that assumes coherence and a complete picture of reality.

11 See Scheurich (1996) for a further discussion of these points.

1 The life of theory

The simple act of telling a woman's story from a woman's point of view is a revolutionary act..

Carol Christ 1986:16

This chapter is itself a life history. It traces my theoretical development to what I now consider a critical, poststructuralist, feminist perspective. By placing myself within this work I hope to avoid the decontextualization and detachment, so often found in social science research, that perpetuate the myth of objectivity and neutrality. In identifying myself as a critical, poststructuralist feminist, I realize that this label is not unproblematic. It creates the illusion that my identity is neatly boxed in a theoretical framework. Like Linda Nicholson (1994:103), I believe that it is necessary to 'explicitly acknowledge that our claims about women are not based on some given reality but emerge from our own places within history and culture; they are political acts that reflect the contexts we emerge out of and the futures we would like to see'. My evolving personal experiences, as well as my theoretical positions, are intimately and subjectively intertwined. Together, they weave the context for understanding this work.

Writing the past of possible futures

From an early age I was aware of my gendered position. Although at the time I did not recognize the systematic ways in which gender differences were produced, I knew that to be male was more highly valued than to be female. My 'resistance' to being devalued was to emulate male ways of knowing and being. My high school yearbook lists my future profession as 'lawyer'. I embraced the liberal feminist ideology of the 1970s, which suggested that ending women's oppression would come as a result of equality. While an undergraduate, I enrolled in a women's studies course. At that time I was exposed to Simone de Beauvoir's (1953) *The Second Sex* and Betty Friedan's (1974) *The Feminine Mystique*. Through these readings I was able to name and articulate my experiences of devaluation, and identify the ways in which traditional female roles were socially constructed. Kate Millet (1970) and Betty Friedan (1974), as Dorothy Smith (1987:50) points out, 'unveiled the rupture between women's experience and the ideological nature of the values, norms and beliefs concerning women's roles and the relations between the sexes which had been taken for granted'.

In making explicit how the differences in socialization resulted in unequal opportunities I understood that the inequality of men and women was the product of gender socialization, and not the result of innate biological characteristics. Consequently, it seemed that for women equality was only a matter of stepping out of our traditional roles and gaining access to the positions of power usually occupied by men. Liberation seemed around the corner, or so I thought. Resistance, in the case of liberal feminism, insisted that subjective transformation was a major site of political change (Henriques *et al.* 1984). Although criticized by the left as bourgeois and individualistic, the focus on personal change challenged traditional forms of resistance, which restricted social transformation to the public sphere of protest and revolution that traditionally excluded women. If liberation merely meant the access of women to the spheres previously controlled by men, then one of the major shortcomings of liberal feminism was the lack of critique of the social institutions, and the resultant structures of knowledge, that held privileged positions (Pinar *et al.* 1995). That these forms of knowledge were gendered, and thus functioned to continue to dismiss women's experience and knowledge as legitimate, was a realization that did not come easily.

My awareness of the Euro-American, heterosexual, middle-class bias of liberal feminism came by way of an unusual detour. As part of my major studies in post-colonial African history I was introduced to novels such as Chinua Achebe's (1959) *Things Fall Apart*, Ousmane Sembene's (1962) *God's Bits of Wood* and James Ngugi's (1964) *Weep Not, Child*, along with what I then termed more theoretical writings, such as Frantz Fanon's (1961) *The Wretched of the Earth*, Paulo Freire's (1973) *Pedagogy of the Oppressed* and works by Julius Nyrere and Kwami Nkrumah.[1] Their critique of Eurocentrism had a powerful impact on my understandings of the world. I began to question the Eurocentric bias of history; the ethnocentrism inherent in the values, beliefs and norms with which I had been raised; and perhaps most importantly, the role of capitalism in the exploitation of Third World people, particularly women.

My seduction by resistance theory thus had its origins in Marxist and reproduction theories, which located the structures of oppression, and consequently change, in economic relations of power.[2] As a result, I turned to the writings of Karl Marx and Mao Tse-tung in order to gain a deeper understanding of the systematic ways in which social, political and economic structures reproduced the interests of white, upper-class, Euro-Americans. Reproduction theory, with its roots in Marxian analysis of social oppression, appealed to me. According to Marx, it was not the consciousness of men (*sic*) that determined their existence, but their social existence that determined their consciousness. In rejecting liberal accounts of human change as embedded in the individual's capacity for rational, autonomous thought and actions, Marx proposed that the relations of production generate a superstructure of legal, political and social ideas that regulate society and shape individuals. At the same time, my feminist sensibilities warned me that the roots of sexual oppression lay deeper than the structures of capitalism and would not disappear as a result of a proletarian revolution.

As I struggled to come to grips with the contradictory ideals and values of an upper-middle-class, white suburban upbringing and my emerging political awakening through my studies in African history, I went to Ghana, West Africa for a term. I was surprised that Ghanaian women did not perceive themselves as victims of patriarchy. My experiences with Ghanaian women who saw themselves as exploited more by US capitalism than by males in their own communities, forced me to re-evaluate the assumptions I had made about the universal experiences of patriarchy. I became disturbed by the rigid categories of class, race and gender, which neglected the interrelatedness of these categories in understanding oppression.

Although categories like class and gender heightened my understandings of systematic oppression, these categories also got in the way of seeing the complex and contradictory ways in which reproduction and resistance functioned. What I found particularly disturbing was the deterministic nature of a materialist analysis. Like Kathy Davis and Sue Fisher (1993), I found that reducing an understanding of social relations to a structural analysis limited the modes of resistance by focusing primarily on the way that power oppresses, thus excluding the notion of personal agency. Positing capitalism and patriarchy as the sole culprits of women's subordination 'leaves little conceptual or political space for uncovering the subtle and ambivalent ways women may be negotiating at the margins of power, sometimes constrained by but also resisting and even undermining asymmetrical power structures' (Davis and Fisher 1993:6).

The location of power solely in macrostructures situates resistance in a binary world in which the oppressed (powerless) struggle against the oppressor (powerful). Despite the radical nature of Marxism as a theory of social change, it is deeply embedded in humanist notions of subjectivity, power and change. Change is defined within modernist terms in which progress is linear, incremental and progressive rather than recursive and transformative (Doll 1993). The dichotomy between liberation or oppression set up in Marxist theories of social change has traditionally functioned, according to Bettina Aptheker (1989:171),

> to situate women, if they have been seen at all, as objects of oppression: either as victims of circumstances to be rescued, educated, and brought into productive and public life; or as the backward and misguided pawns of reactionary (or counterrevolutionary) forces to be won over

to progressive and revolutionary movements. In neither case are women seen as an autonomous, purposeful, active force in history.

Despite the allure of the neat metanarrative of Marxism, in which power resides primarily in the state or economy, as a feminist I was concerned with the overly reductionist nature of Marxism's tendency to overlook the individual subject as an agent of change capable of conscious, critical thought (Gramsci 1971; Wexler 1976; Willis 1977; Apple 1979; Anyon 1983). Unfortunately, the Marxist division of the world into the powerless and powerful, the oppressor and oppressed, the emancipator and those needing emancipation, reproduced the very binaries, central to patriarchy, that I, as a feminist, sought to disrupt.

With these theoretical debates whirling round and round, I entered the state schools as a secondary social studies teacher with the intention of raising the consciousness of students and bringing about social change. This was a political choice with the following goals: to empower students, in particular women and minorities, to recognize their own oppression; to integrate women's history and social history into the curriculum; and to teach US history from a non-Eurocentric perspective in order to raise students' awareness of the USA's role in the exploitation and oppression of Third World people. I saw myself as an active agent for change, not as a teacher. I was a political activist who happened to be a teacher. With Howard Zinn's (1980) *A People's History of the United States*, I disposed of the traditional textbook and headed into the classroom.

Unlearning teacher as revolutionary

During my five years of teaching (1983–8), my own sense of agency was often at odds with the educational trends towards increased control and bureaucratization. I vividly remember my first in-service day in the autumn of 1983. A summary of *Nation at Risk* (National Commission of Excellence in Education 1983) was given to the eight hundred teachers in our district. According to this report American education was in a crisis. Excellence in education, attributed to equity in the 1960s and 1970s, shifted to a focus on excellence characterized by social efficiency, which sought to address low worker productivity and the declining economic edge of the USA in the world economy (Feinberg 1993). This 'crisis', as Kathleen Weiler (1993:216) suggests, is part of a larger global shift in educational policies that 'attack the ideals of equality and justice'. Educational policies in Great Britain (Arnot 1993), New Zealand (Middleton 1993) and Australia (Yates 1993) are characterized by,

> striking similarities, calling for educational policies to meet the needs of business, increasing standardization and control over teachers' work,

and encouraging moves toward two-tiered educational systems which would protect the interests of the groups who hold power, and legitimate the educational 'failure' of a growing class of low paid service workers composed largely of white women and men and women of color.

(Weiler 1993:217)

These supposed 'reforms' not only maintained that the primary role of education was to serve economic needs, but they regulated gender through the discourse of professionalization. Professionalization in this context meant transforming teaching in several ways: from an undifferentiated occupation to a stratified one; from a field based on an ambiguous body of knowledge to a science of teaching; and from a *laissez-faire* approach of teacher authority to a standardized vision of teaching practice.[3]

My ongoing ambivalence about entering a profession considered to be 'women's work' was initially eased by the talk of 'professionalizing teaching'. The discourse of professionalism offers the female teacher, according to Larabee (1992:132), 'a way to escape identification with the unpaid and uncredentialed status of the mother'. In taking up the identity of a 'professional', I saw myself to be resisting the gendered nature and traditional devaluation of teaching as women's work. In hindsight, my resistance functioned in complex ways to subvert the essentialized nature of the teaching profession while simultaneously reproducing masculinist gender norms such as rationality, autonomy and individuality associated with 'professionalism'. Rather than see this as a moment of false consciousness, I now understand that my investment in the discourse of professionalism made it possible for me to construct an identity in which I could become a teacher. Taking up that identity also led to my eventual criticism of 'professionalism' as a discourse that functioned to degender teaching. As Barbara Beatty (1990) suggests, professionalism imposes masculine models of work and career advancement, which privilege autonomy, hierarchy and segmentation. My experience 'trying on' professionalism highlighted the way that subjectivities shaped through discourse can function at one moment as liberatory and the next as oppressive. Thus, resistance and agency were not unitary concepts that could be applied in a recipe-like fashion, but specific context-dependent discursive moments in my 'lived experience' that functioned in complex and contradictory ways. When I read Foucault (1980) I knew what he meant by the assertion that everything was dangerous. As a consequence, the poststructuralist call to give up grand narratives of liberation and unitary theories of oppression, although difficult for me, made sense when I saw the contradictions in my own experience.

The irony was that at the time professionalism was being stressed, there were increased efforts to control the teaching profession. Outcomes Based Education (OBE) was introduced in my second year of teaching. This educational reform, like the movement to 'professionalize' teaching, constructed teacher subjectivity in conflicting ways. The outcomes for learning were generated through the collaborative efforts of teachers, but once the outcomes were generated, accountability measures implemented through standardized tests were used to determine the 'effectiveness' of each of the teachers. Any gains in collaboration were outweighed by the competition among teachers for the highest test scores. Ironically, collaboration functioned to situate teachers as 'agents charged with policing one another's oppression' (Smyth 1991:95).

The rigid adherence to outcomes, 'one a day' (of course, written on the board), threatened to undermine any possibility of an emergent curriculum or student-centred classroom. My curriculum was increasingly criticized for being 'too soft'. Teaching the histories of women, Native Americans and other minority groups was considered 'enrichment', and not the core or 'basic' curriculum.[4] I learned to close the door so the administrators would not notice all the group work I did; it was not considered real teaching. My group work, role playing and simulations were discounted as 'fun' but not real learning. 'Real learning', they believed, only took place during lectures. Eventually, I felt alienated, frustrated and unwilling to compromise my values one more time. Although my work with students had been rewarding, the increased lack of autonomy, the devaluation of my work and the hierarchical nature of the schools made it difficult to maintain my level of commitment. I needed to understand the competing pressures and counterpressures I had experienced as I strived to be politically committed. How could schools be sites of social change, and more specifically, how could teachers resist the deskilling taking place through current reforms (Apple 1979)?

(Re)schooled: making sense of theory

After five years of teaching, disillusioned by the realization that state schools were not sites for promoting real change, I sought to make a difference in another arena; teacher education. I re-entered graduate school and found that the assumptions of my critical perspective, which had maintained that I could empower students and raise their consciousness, were severely shaken. My focus on emancipating students revealed my assumptions of power as a commodity, which I had, and they did not. This understanding of power reified notions of subjectivity as unitary and resistance as opposition. These taken-for-granted ways of thinking underscored not only the vestiges of liberal ideology, but Marxism's complicity in enlightenment thought. As I began my doctoral course work in 1988 I learned that the hegemony of Marxism as a radical discourse had been interrupted by a number of sociopolitical movements. These included feminism as well as interpretivist and phenomenological movements (Greene 1975; Pinar 1975), all of which opened up new possibilities for understandings of subjectivity and resistance. Reproduction theory, with its focus on determining the 'origins' of social oppression, was itself criticized as reproducing patriarchy (Pinar 1983).[5]

I found that a phenomenological framework highlighted the social individual by acknowledging that humans act in a world of meaning that they encounter and help to create, renegotiate and sustain. In focusing on the 'lived experience' and 'agency' of social actors, the role of the individual in negotiating and resisting hegemonic forces was highlighted. By placing the individual and her interpretive and negotiating capacities at the centre of analysis, those engaged in phenomenological critique rejected the reduction of the subject to passivity, as well as notions of false consciousness and economic determinism.[6] What remains problematic in this framework is the potential romanticization of the individual, which reinforces the traditional view of an autonomous self free from the material forces of social structures.

This romanticization of the individual was unsettling to me, as a feminist, because it deflected the role of social structures such as patriarchy. Seeking some resolution (I still thought I could achieve one), I turned to the work of neo-Marxists, production theorists and critical theorists such as Althusser (1971), Habermas (1976) and Adorno (1973), who rejected the notion of a single, central apparatus of control (Bourdieu 1977). They rejected the binary that situated power either as property of the individual (phenomenologists) or as imposed by macrostructures (Marxists) by focusing on how ideology and culture (as well as economic hegemony) reproduce existing power relations through the production and distribution of a dominant culture (Giroux 1983). In particular, the work of Gramsci (1971) suggested how structural determinants were not static, but were continually being reimposed and were thus capable of being resisted by historical subjects. Those influenced by Gramsci (Williams 1977), recognized the importance of the concept of ideology in understanding power and resistance. This worked to undermine rigid distinctions between cultural, social, economic and political processes (Abu-Lughod 1990). Thus, resistance took its shape in the alternative cultural and political institutions created by the oppressed as a means of understanding, opposing and changing their position. Neo-Marxists charged that it was the distribution of knowledge and its legitimation, rather than the acquisition of specific values and behaviours, that was central to understanding reproduction (Bernstein 1975; Apple 1979).

Production theorists (Wexler 1976; Apple 1979; Giroux 1983), who stressed the power of individuals to come to a critical consciousness of their own world, stressed the dialectic between individual consciousness and structural determinants. Mechanisms of reproduction are never complete and always meet with opposition. This concept of resistance was central to critical theorists' understanding of the complex interaction between agency and structure. Critical educational theorists adopted the concept of resistance to highlight the complexity of the relationship between individual consciousness and structural determinants. The work of critical, neo-Marxists (Willis 1977; Anyon 1983; Stanley 1992) further highlighted the complexities of resistance by suggesting that what might appear to be genuine instances of resistance have had the long-term effect of reproducing, at a deeper level, the dominant order. This focus on the complex forms of resistance interrupted static and bound understandings by acknowledging the fluid and contradictory ways in which resistance could function.

The impact of production theory or the 'new sociology' on education emerged in its practical sub-discourse of 'critical pedagogy'. Advocates of critical pedagogy are dedicated to producing emancipatory knowledge, which has as its goal the 'conscious empowerment' of the oppressed to change their exploitative situations (Freire 1973; Apple 1978, 1979; Comstock 1982; Giroux 1986; McLaren 1989). Central to a critical perspective is the assumption that oppressed persons are not 'empowered', or 'conscious'. Implicit in the notion of empowerment is the assumption that someone needs to be empowered. Although a critical perspective is attractive because it focuses on resistance and emancipation, thereby addressing the feminist goal of ending oppression, the question of who determines the knowledge and action necessary to eliminate oppression remains unresolved.

As I reflected on my decision to enter teaching, in which I had constructed my subjectivity as a 'change agent', it became clear that my position simultaneously functioned to reproduce and resist dominant ideologies. My own initial notion of empowering students through reeling off tales of the oppressed perpetuated, in many ways, a 'banking' model of teaching. By giving them the 'right' story, indoctrinating them with the 'facts', they would be awakened to the 'truth'. In other words, I still believed that 'knowledge' would set them free. It was distressing when the young women in my US history class showed little interest in my carefully prepared slide presentation of 'women in the west'. Were they already victims of false consciousness? Why were these young women so resistant to my attempts to 'empower' them?

That many of these young women clearly understood unequal power relations and sought to combat them became clear to me only when I reluctantly agreed to be sponsor for the wrestling cheerleaders. In taking up this role I saw my actions as contributing to the oppression of these girls as sexual objects, thus furthering the aims of patriarchy. Carmen, Cecilia and Adrienne were not the blonde, blue-eyed prototypes of the football cheerleading squad, yet for them, becoming cheerleaders functioned as an act of resistance and agency to the normative discourses of femininity. They clearly understood the status differential between their squad and the football cheerleaders. In being cheerleaders they took up the traditional role of women as supporters of men and objects of men's gaze; at the same time these particular girls contested the assumption that only blonde, middle-class girls could be cheerleaders. Their astute perceptions and analyses of unequal class relations and how gender norms of femininity affected them provided me with an alternative way to read their classroom behaviour.[7] This disruption of my original understandings of resistance, the beginning of the blurring of concepts like resistance, power and agency, I credit to the teachings of the wrestling cheerleaders, or as they were commonly called, the 'mat maids'. My understanding that resistance is not fixed, but always contingent on the form and analysis of power, dislodged my ability to assume what constituted resistance and, more importantly, my beliefs that I 'knew' how to 'liberate' my students from oppression.

The very agency of individuals to resist, claimed by feminists and critical theorists, seems undermined by talk of the need to 'empower' and 'emancipate' (Ellsworth 1989; Orner 1992; Gore 1993). My wanting to 'empower' the students, although giving the illusion of equality, in effect leaves intact an authoritarian relationship. Angela McRobbie (1982:52) asks, 'How can we assume that they need anything done for them in the first place? Or conversely, that we have anything real to offer them?' By dividing the world into tidy categories of 'oppressed' and 'non-oppressed', the liberatory discourses of both critical theorists and feminists actually reified a modernist view of power as a possession, which I had and the oppressed did not. This hierarchy positioned me, the teacher, as the emancipator and my students as needing emancipation. The oppressive power relations I criticized as a feminist ironically were reproduced through my taking up the subject position of a critical pedagogue. That critical theory was implicated in the production and maintenance of patriarchy soon became clear to me.

The notion of 'liberating' or 'empowering' students, implicit in my understanding of myself as 'change agent', underscored how critical theory was still embedded in humanist conceptions of a unitary subject, and thus ultimately gendered as male. Although knowledge is no longer understood in a positivist sense as neutral or objective within critical, neo-Marxist theory, the concept of knowledge as resistance or emancipation still assumes an inherently human essence waiting to be liberated from an unjust, imposed power structure. As Valerie Walkerdine (1990:9) points out, central to these theories is the notion of the individual as a 'real and essential kernel of phenomenological Marxism, whose outer skins are just a series of roles which can be cast off to reveal the true and revolutionary self'. As a feminist, this understanding of resistance is particularly problematic due specifically to the romanticism of the individual, which is allied to an ideology of the heroic, and consequently understood as male.

The very concept of liberation embedded in critical theory, is, as Kathleen Weiler (1991) suggests, deeply implicated in an androcentric world view, because of the universal and abstract nature in which oppression is theorized. Critical theory's goals of opposing oppression and seeking liberation are in themselves universal truths that, according to Weiler (1991:450), 'do not address the specificity of people's lives; they do not directly analyze the contradictions between conflicting oppressed groups or the ways in which a single individual can experience oppression in one sphere while being privileged or oppressive in another'. The assumption that there is a collective experience of oppression that can be named, obscures difference, especially in regard to gender and race.

Feminists working from a cross-cultural–poststructuralist perspective (Minh-ha 1987; Spivak 1987; Christian 1988; Narayan 1988; Spelman 1988; hooks 1989; Anzaldua 1990) have been particularly critical of the oppressive and impositional nature of 'universal' theorizing by highlighting the ways in which concepts like oppression, empowerment and liberation are inherently culture-bound and thus dismiss alternative forms of resistance. The rejection of universal categories that theorize gender, oppression and other social relations has not only challenged conceptions of a single 'womanhood', but also the very possibility of a unified theory of oppression. Refusal to validate univocal interpretations of experience has generated a new appreciation of plurality and has stimulated creative thinking about ways to value difference (Hawkesworth 1989).

By making problematic universal notions of oppression, power and knowledge, women of colour and feminists have not only disrupted Cartesian definitions of the universal male, white subject, but have sought to dislodge what are considered real and legitimate ways of knowing and being. In particular, they have highlighted the tendency of critical and feminist theories to remain grounded in a liberal, humanist tradition in which reason and rationality are the privileged ways of coming to know.[8] This is perhaps nowhere more apparent than in the assumption of critical theories that through dialogue those involved in transformative pedagogy will come to a common understanding of the roots of oppression and the goals of liberation. According to Elizabeth Ellsworth (1989:316), critical theory functions as repressive through 'conventional notions of dialogue and democracy which assume rationalized, individualized subjects capable of agreeing on universal fundamental moral principles and the quality of human life'. By privileging dialogue, reason and universality, critical theory functioned to normalize experience as male. In essence, taking up resistance theory functioned as a masculinist discourse that posited subjectivity as male and unitary. In this regard, critical theory was no longer 'liberatory' for me. In effect, resistance theory simultaneously constructed a subject position in which I was both oppresser and oppressed.

Like other educators (Luke and Gore 1992; Casey 1993; Jipson *et al.* 1995), I struggled with how to continue to work for social change without violating the rights of others to construct their own knowledge. My perception of the teacher as social change agent and my understandings of resistance had been challenged in numerous ways. I resonated with critical theorists' understanding of the complex interaction between agency and structure. In particular the ethnographic study *Learning to Labour* (Willis 1977), which highlighted the role that resistance and negotiation played in the lives of young working-class English lads, made sense to me based on my experiences with the wrestling cheerleaders. In his study, Willis rejects earlier theories of deviance as an explanation of anti-authority behaviour.[9] Rather, he viewed acts previously labelled as deviant as acts of resistance against the dominant culture, which had exploited and devalued them. At the same time, the acts of resistance in which these lads engaged eventually resulted in the reproduction of their class positions. Like the young women who became wrestling cheerleaders, acts of resistance *both* reproduced and contested gender norms.

Despite this more complex view of resistance by critical theorists, as a feminist I continued to be disturbed by the understanding of resistance as a concept that was unitary, conceptualized as opposed to power and embedded in male experience. How could my support of the wrestling cheerleaders be theorized as resistance within feminist and critical theory? From a feminist perspective, my support of the cheerleaders would be seen as capitulating to patriarchy. At best, from a critical perspective, my support would be seen as 'false consciousness'. I wondered about the forms of resistance that remained obscured by grand theories and metanarratives of change. Simultaneously, when resistance theory did not take the male experience as normative, what would resistance look like? How might we theorize resistance if we took seriously women teachers' lives and experiences? In essence, my emerging dissertation research conducting life histories with women teachers became a way to validate my own experiences and name them.

As I embarked on this research, I little knew that my focus on resistance would in fact lead to a radical rethinking of notions of identity, subjectivity and agency. Ultimately these women teachers' narratives did not reveal 'acts' of resistance. Instead, the modes of self-representation embedded in their life history narratives suggested the complex ways in which they negotiated understandings of self against and with/in the dominant discourses of education and gender. In taking women educators' narratives seriously as a site for theory construction I was continually amazed at how their stories exemplified the theories of poststructuralism. Theories of non-unitary subjectivity, of power as circulatory and agency as contradictory took on meanings within these women's stories. I stopped trying to fit their stories into my theories and listened. The more I did this the more I was able to hear. Their narratives led me to further reject grand theories and pushed me to think about resistance, power and agency in more complex ways. This prompting resulted in my immersion in poststructural theory. Still clinging to my commitment to teaching as a form of political activism and social change, I struggled to be open to theories that undermined the very foundations of critical theory and its unitary notions of change, power and the subject.

Without these, I thought, how could there be social transformation? In the following sections I trace my grapplings with the tensions between critical, feminist and poststructural theory. I see these theoretical discussions as central to the lives of women teachers, and the lives of women teachers as central to informing these theoretical debates.

Engendering resistance theory: poststructural–feminist perspectives

Attempting to define poststructuralism is perhaps, in itself, a contradiction in terms. Despite differences among various poststructural theories, the common thread is the rejection of grand narratives. Universal or absolute truths, hallmarks of humanist, Enlightenment thought are suspect. Reality is not out there but is constructed through discourse; through language. This deconstruction includes the rejection of a unitary, rational, autonomous subject. A primary concern of poststructuralist thinkers has been to analyse how 'individuals are constituted as subjects and given unified identities or subject positions' (Best and Kellner 1991:24). While there is agreement that the subject is a product of humanist discourse, there is much debate about how the subject is constituted. In true poststructuralist style, there are multiple narratives, ranging from what Seyla Benhabib (1995) has termed weak to strong 'versions' of the 'Death of Man'. In the strong version, in which I would situate Derrida and Lacan, the subject is primarily the product of discourse/language. In fact there is no subject; the subject 'dissolves into a chain of significations' (Benhabib 1995:20). Foucault's version of poststructuralism shifts attention to how the subject is not solely the product of language, but that institutions such as prisons, hospitals and asylums (and I would include schools) produce relations of power and knowledge that regulate and constitute the subject. My own version of poststructuralism draws heavily on Foucault, due to what I see as the ruptures and possibilities he provides for rethinking agency and resistance. However, to take up poststructuralism, and in particular Foucault, has not been unproblematic for me. Although I now consider myself to be and call myself a feminist poststructuralist, this claiming of a position is not without its ambiguity, reservations or concerns. As a feminist I don't fear that poststructuralism necessarily results in a lack of intentionality or agency. On the contrary, I believe that it offers possibilities for reconceiving the subject, resistance and agency in more complex and powerful ways. However, I take to heart Foucault's admonition that everything is dangerous (1980). No knowledge is free of power relations, and poststructuralism is no exception. Consequently, before I discuss at length how poststructuralism can in fact produce a subject with agency, I discuss some of the concerns feminists have voiced in regard to various versions of poststructuralism. My own discomfort in embracing poststructuralism, despite the 'liberatory' ways in which it has disrupted the universal subject, are ongoing and continually in flux. I do not want to smooth over the contradictions and tensions I experience as I continue to struggle to situate myself in the life of theory.

Although my dissertation drew heavily on poststructural notions of subjectivity as non-unitary, of power/knowledge as circulatory and of gender as a complex social construction, it was by no means an uncontested Foucauldian work. I struggled with claiming a feminist position while simultaneously valorizing yet another male theorist. In fact, I remember distinctly a session at the Conference of Curriculum Theorizing led by Elizabeth Ellsworth and Mimi Orner on women's experiences of academia. It was an alternative session in which we were encouraged to re-present our experiences in some visual fashion. I drew the red circle with a slash through Foucault. Why, I struggled to understand, were feminists buying into another grand narrative? And why were we still raiding the 'master's' toolbox, even though I suspect most feminists agreed that the 'master's tools will never dismantle the master's house' (Lorde 1984:110)?

On some level I also questioned why Foucault was getting all the credit for poststructuralism when it seemed to me that on some level women and other marginalized groups had been engaging in deconstruction in some form or another for quite some time. Wasn't Charlotte Perkins Gilman's Utopian novel *Herland* (1979) in which she laid bare how turn-of-the-century gender discourses structured power and knowledge as male, a deconstruction of the biological essentialism of mothering? Zora Neal Hurston's novels, in particular *Mules and Men* (1969), disrupted concepts central to the emerging discipline of anthropology. She played with authorial voice, notions of objectivity and subjectivity, and the power relations reproduced in the colonial relationship of the anthropologist and 'his' or 'her' people. Rejecting traditional anthropological writing by taking up fiction was in itself a criticism of the binaries of fact and fiction and the 'disciplining of knowledge' through supposed scientific, objective methods. To suggest that Foucault was somehow the 'founding father' of poststructuralism is to participate in the production of another grand, neat, tidy metanarrative in which progress once again followed a sequential, neat, linear story of enlightenment that went from liberal humanist thought, through Marxism (and its subtheories of feminism and postcolonial theory) to poststructuralism.[10] The irony was that this reproduced the very kind of grand narrative deconstruction criticized. Concepts like progress, false consciousness and grand theories of liberation seemed nowhere more apparent than in some versions of poststructuralism. What was particularly disturbing was that despite poststructuralism's focus on difference, it potentially functioned to obscure the work of women of colour and other feminists.

As Jana Sawicki (1991:9) suggests,

The political critique of feminist theory that originated among black, poor and third world women gave a flesh and blood significance to poststructuralist accounts of the suppression of difference in the constitution of identity that was much more compelling than any philosophical arguments could ever produce.

Consequently, despite my discomfort in the contradictory ways that poststructuralism was working, I was compelled by the work of poststructuralist feminists and women of colour, who highlighted the potential of poststructural theory to disrupt the unitary subject and thus reconceptualize resistance. In the following sections I trace my immersion in feminist and poststructuralist theories as I struggled to understand their implications for rethinking resistance.

Rethinking resistance: poststructural perspectives

For feminists, resistance is a slippery construct in which we grapple with the need to claim a position as a subject, resisting our erasure, while recognizing that the very appropriation of subjecthood reifies the category of subject that has been essential to patriarchy (Gilmore 1994; Jacobs *et al.* 1995). The poststructuralist freeing of the 'subject' in which subjectivity is seen as non-unitary, multiple and constantly in flux is central to deconstructing the universal male subject of liberal, humanist as well as neo-Marxist discourse (Henriques *et al.* 1984). Yet, to what degree does the notion of subjectivity, in which individuals actively choose from multiple and often conflicting discourses, merely act as a new and more accurate 'truth' claim? Feminist critics suggest that it is, perhaps, no accident that at the very time feminists and others obtained a subject, the subject became non-unitary. As Nancy Hartstock (1990:163) asks, 'Why is it that just at the moment when so many of us who have been silenced begin to demand the right to name ourselves, as subjects, rather than as objects of history, that just then the concept of subjecthood becomes problematic?'[11] In what ways does the creation of a new subject, albeit non-unitary, perpetuate discursive practices that reify a universal reality central to modernist thought?

Positioning resistance within these larger ideological, political struggles in which feminists struggle to account for the specificity of gender/subjectivity without falling either into an essentialized discourse or lapsing into relativism highlights the insidious hegemony of binary modernist discourse (Whitson 1991).[12] Accordingly, I am reluctant to reduce current feminist theorizing to the dualistic tension reproduced in the essentialism–relativism debate. In fact, this simplistic dichotomy merely recreates the binary view of the world that I, as a feminist, seek to disrupt. Like Patti Lather (1991:30), I maintain that feminism 'becomes not a veering between the passive, dispersed subject of deconstruction on the one hand, and, on the other hand, the transcendent subject of most emancipatory discourse, but the site of the systematic fighting-out of that instability'. It is in the site of that 'fighting-out' that new considerations of resistance must be explored.

Women's experience of resistance must first and foremost be understood from their position as objects. As Bettina Aptheker (1989:173) suggests,

> Women's resistance comes out of women's subordinated status to men, institutionalized in society and lived through every day in countless personal ways. Women's resistance is not necessarily or intrinsically oppositional; it is not necessarily or intrinsically contesting for power. It does however, have a profound impact on the fabric of social life because of its steady, cumulative effects. It is central to the making of history, and . . . it is the bedrock of social change.

Two points are central to my argument. Women have resisted and women's resistance is shaped primarily and fundamentally by our position as objects. Because women have traditionally been defined as objects, Nancy Miller (1989) maintains that women's relation to integrity and textuality, to desire and authority and, thus, to resistance displays structurally important differences from the universal concept of resistance claimed by patriarchy.[13] It is from this standpoint, in which the very naming of ourselves as subjects is an act of resistance, that this book explores how women teachers constitute their subjectivity through and in their life history narratives.

So how can we rethink resistance? In light of the poststructuralist assertion that 'where there is power, there is resistance' (Foucault 1978:95–6), is resistance an obsolete notion?[14] Two notions seem to me to be central to the traditional concept of resistance. Resistance is defined in terms of opposition and power. Opposition implies force, and this, according to Bettina Aptheker (1989:170), is counterposed to accommodation or collaboration. This excludes the possibility that accommodation, in the form of taking up or complying with dominant ideologies, can also function as a form of subversion or disruption. Traditionally the rejection of dominant ideologies has constituted 'resistance'. However, when power is reconceived as not primarily repressive, but as a constellation dispersed within specific microlevel contexts, resistance is reduced not merely to opposition but also appropriation of or the taking up of dominant ideologies. Trinh Minh-ha (1991:17) has suggested that, in engaging dominant ideologies while simultaneously disrupting them, women 'narrate a displacement as they relentlessly shuttle between the center (patriarchal norms) and the margins (their own understandings)'. Thus, resistance is not limited only to the use of nonhegemonic discourses, for hegemonic discourses can also be reconfigured and deployed to subvert each other (Hekman 1995). What was previously interpreted as 'false consciousness' takes on new meanings when resistance is understood as mobile and transitory. Because multiple centres of power confront multiple centres of resistance, supposedly liberatory discourses such as feminism and Marxism can function as an instrument of domination or, as Gore (1993) maintains, a 'regime of truth'. Likewise a hegemonic discourse can be taken up or performed as a liberatory discourse.

I came to understand the complexity of resistance through collaborating with four other women (Jipson *et al.* 1995) over the course of a four-year project in which we grappled with the implications of feminism, critical theory and postmodernism for our practices as teachers. Over two years, meeting as a research-study group, we continually sought to understand our differences despite our common commitment to teaching as a form of social change. While I embraced feminism as my primary form of resistance, Gretchen, an Ojibiwa-Winnebego, experienced feminism as an extension of white, Western, colonial thought. Susan, the daughter of Holocaust survivors, always understood her experiences first as a Jew and only second as a woman. For Jan, class came first, then gender, and for Karen categories of gender, class, race and ethnicity were all constructs deeply embedded in Western, Cartesian thought. Experiencing this multiplicity of perspectives on power relations, emancipatory politics and the role of theory pushed me to rethink my deeply embedded assumptions regarding resistance.

Traditional conceptions of resistance assume that power is defined as political power, which can be acquired, seized or shared. These universalized definitions of resistance as political–public and oppositional, are firmly grounded in patriarchal understandings of power as identifiable and, thus, contestable. The corollary assumption that change is linear and incremental has similarly functioned to exclude women's forms of resistance. These understandings of power differ markedly from those in which 'meaning can be political only when it does not let itself be easily stabilized and when it does not rely on any single source of authority, but rather empties it, or decentralizes it' (Minh-ha 1991:41). An understanding of resistance based on positionality (Alcoff 1989) acknowledges subjectivity as non-unitary and continually in flux, yet does not exclude the agency of the subject. For women, the decentring of the subject has served as a primary form of resistance. I understand Maxine Greene (1992) when she suggests that women's understanding of subjectivity as non-unitary signifies a form of subversion to patriarchy.

While Greene sees the loss of the subject as creating possibilities for understanding women's forms of resistance, some feminist theorists have seen the loss of the subject as an undermining of the political project of feminism. Because these theoretical arguments are political, as well as central to my interpretation of the cultural politics of resistance in women teachers' narratives, in the following sections I review in greater depth the divergent feminist standpoints on the implications of the 'loss of the subject' for feminist theorizing.

Feminist theory without a subject

The primary concern of feminists in regard to poststructuralist theory has been the lack of a theory of resistance (Grimshaw 1993). Without a subject, how could there be agency? In other words, without the category 'women', how can there be feminism? The poststructural argument that knowledge is not universal, but rather produced from a particular 'standpoint', has raised, among feminists, the question of whether poststructuralism leads to a relativism that ultimately undermines theoretical and/or political action (Harding 1987). Some feminists (Alcoff 1989; Flax 1989; Mascia-Lees *et al.* 1989) have pointed out the potential of a poststructural perspective to exclude women by relativizing all experience, thus undermining the basis for an adequate feminist politics. Foucault's emphasis on the dangers of identity formation can, according to Sawicki (1991:105) all 'too easily become the basis for repudiating women's struggles'.

For some, the decentralization of the subject potentially precludes acts of agency and resistance. Jane Flax (1990:217) cautions that the subject that is always in flux, constantly remaking itself, 'presupposes a socially isolated and individualistic view of the self'. This understanding of subjectivity relegates agency to a kind of 'discourse determinism' in which there is little or no room for resistance (Henriques *et al.* 1984). If experience is solely the product of discourse (shaped through language), does this re-invoke determinism and deny the subject the ability to reflect and contest social discourse? What are the implications of this discourse determinism for the feminist project? What happens when the worlds of women are treated as texts, as systems of signs that resist decoding because of the multiplicities of meaning (Moi 1985; Hawkesworth 1989)?

Mahoney and Yngnesson (1992:52), critiquing a Lacanian 'strong version' of the 'death of man', maintain that what is needed to avoid the discourse determinism of poststructuralism is an 'explanation of how specific actors come to take on individual identities', which 'requires some attention to them as engaged in relationship, not simply positioned as performers or spectators'. In other words, they caution that current Lacanian-derived psychological explanations of subjectivity constituted by contradictory identities, although promising, are inadequate to explain resistance because they describe a fundamentally asocial subject, and thus miss the crucial relational ground for the subject's experience of such contradictions. The potential danger to feminists of this slide into relativism is the fictive element. Our stories become fictions; stories among many other stories. Our experiences of oppression as women – rape, domestic violence and sexual harassment – are easily interpreted as fictions; distortions of our reality.[15] We become subject to fiction.

In addition to the real, material, political consequences of conceptualizing the subject as a product of discourse, there is also an epistemological issue.

Limiting experience or subjectivity as solely shaped by discourse (primarily masculinist and phallocentric constructs) limits the experiences that women can articulate. Discourse determinism limits modes of representation to language while ignoring the extra-discursive modes of representation or non-representation in which humans engage. That representation is limited to language has itself been argued as a masculinist construction of reality by feminists such as Cixous, Irigaray and Kristeva. As Irigaray and Kristeva have argued, phallocentric discourses offer no place for women to speak.

In raising the question 'Is it possible to have an experience without a knowledge to have it in?', Maureen Cain (1993:85) contests the monolithic assumptions of language as the sole determiner of experience.[16] In limiting women's experiences to discourse, while simultaneously acknowledging that language has been predominately a masculinist construction, Cain (1993) has argued that women's knowledge is inevitably subjugated or repressed. The exclusion of unthinkable experiences or unthought relationships highlights Foucault's lack of attention to the 'differential impact on the lives of men and women of the disciplining procedures to which he does attend' (Soper 1993:39).[17]

Of most concern to me as a feminist is what Cain (1993) has termed the 'ontological primacy' accorded to Foucault. In reducing experience primarily to a product of discourse, Foucault's theories not only function as androcentric, but ironically remain bounded by a set of oppositions whose inevitability it does not question. This oppositional mode of thinking is inevitably gendered or, to put it another way, ignores the role of gender in shaping experience. By ignoring gender it has been argued that Foucault retains something of the universalizing approach to humanity for which he criticized liberal–humanist and Marxist accounts of power. This suggests that gender is not merely one of many floating signifiers for feminist theorizing about concepts of resistance, agency and power. As Sarah Westphal (1994:155) maintains, 'A gendered standpoint is itself a methodological stance, commensurate in its analytical power with Foucauldian methodology. I would argue, therefore, for gender as a theory, along with genealogies of gender.' For de Lauretis (1987), this type of theorizing describes a feminist subject whose awareness of the contradictions of gender identity becomes a 'critical vantage point' providing the creative potential for resistance.

Acknowledging that discourses function simultaneously as liberatory and oppressive, as sites of contradiction in which acts of both resistance and compliance operate, does not necessarily result in the rejection of an identity politics void of power or agency. On the contrary, the complex and contradictory ways in which subjects take up or choose not to take up identities made available to them through discourse become the site for mapping the local and relational dynamics of power and agency. The 'discursive subject', rather than being seen as a passive subject wholly determined by social forces, entails, according to Hekman (1995), subjects finding agency within the discursive spaces open to them in their particular historical period. Agency is a product of discourse, a capacity that flows from a position within discursive formations. The rejection of the unitary subject for a more complex, multiple and contradictory notion of subjectivity results not in a lack of agency but in forms of agency not solely dependent on a universal subject. The non-unitary subject that is in flux, fragmented and decentralized has multiple sites from which to engage in acts of agency. That these acts will work in complex ways to contest and to reify dominant ideologies does not provide cause for consternation, but rather another opportunity to explore the ways in which power works.

My criticisms of poststructuralism, and Foucault in particular, are not a source of disparagement, nor reason for me to reject wholesale the deconstructionist plot (specifically Foucault). On the contrary, taking Foucault seriously means bumping up against the tensions in which he argued that 'everything is dangerous'. He certainly did not, I think, mean to exclude his own theorizing. In fact, within the sites of contradiction the play of power and resistance becomes visible. Thus I turn to what I consider the aspects of poststructuralist theory that enable feminists to rethink notions of subjectivity and, subsequently, power, agency and resistance.

The loss of the subject as increasing sites of resistance

The question for many feminists (Bartky 1990; Sawicki 1991; Hekman 1995; Munro 1996) continues to be, what becomes of resistance and its corollary agency when there is no subject? The appeal of Foucault for me as a feminist is his emphasis on the culturally constructed nature of subjectivity. Notions of the self as unitary, autonomous, universal and static are fictions. Consequently, concepts like man and woman are the product of discourse, and not essentialized categories. The space created within this rupture opened all sorts of possibilities for reconceptualizing agency. When agency is not accorded to a unitary subject – and is always in a state of production – how might women's actions be rethought? For me, this site of production is not cause for despair, but a site of unlimited possibilities for agency. Unrestricted by notions of the subject as unitary, in which one either has power or does not, and in which resistance is dependent on having power, the reconceptualization of the subject as non-unitary allows me to see multiple centres of power confronting multiple centres of resistance. Thus, women are not merely victims of patriarchy, but are also agents, although their acts of resistance need not conform to acts of agency inscribed in primarily patriarchal discourses. This opens up spaces in which to envision the woman teacher as simultaneously rejecting dominant discourses as well as accommodating them. I find this more complex, and often contradictory, position of identity formation ultimately much more comfortable than the notion of a unitary subject, which has functioned as the basis for essentialized notions of woman. Thus, despite my unease over the consequences of the loss of the subject for the political project of feminism, I will explore more specifically the ways in which the 'loss of the subject' provides a rethinking of agency and resistance that can take account of the gendered nature of power.[18]

Rejecting univocal interpretations of experience, feminist poststructuralism shifts the focus of identity politics from the 'woman' subject to how 'woman' is continually constructed through discourse *as* woman. The focus on how discourses create subjects as well as how women resist the constitution of their subjectivity suggests that the subject is constantly in flux. Subjects do not hold power. Power is not a single possession, nor is it located in a unitary, static sense. Power is shifting and fragmentary, relating to positionings given in the apparatuses of regulation themselves (Walkerdine 1990:42). It is everywhere and nowhere. There is no Archimedean point or privileged site of power. It is the construction of these fictions that needs to be deconstructed.[19]

According to Davis and Fisher (1993), power is a 'capillary' circulating through the social body and exerting its authority through self-surveillance and everyday, disciplinary micropractices. Power is dispersed, like a web, with no beginning or end. Frank Pignatelli (1993) suggests that in expanding the surface on which power operates, this dispersion need not lead to despair, but in fact can permit an increase in the amount of power exerted. Although Foucault's dispersal of power and the subject appear to negate the possibility of resistance and political agency, Pignatelli suggests that on the contrary Foucault's reconceptualization of power increases the potential for agency through creating sites in which new forms of identity and subjectivity can continually be invented. By linking power to knowledge through discourse, Davis and Fisher (1993) argue that the focus shifts from the repressive to the productive features of power. Accordingly, 'power produces all social categories, including women, constituting them as both objects and subjects of knowledge' (Davis and Fisher 1993:9). The subject does not vaporize but in fact has a plethora of modes in which to constitute acts of agency. For example, in her ethnographic study of New Jersey waitresses, *Dishing it Out*, Greta Paules (1991) suggests that rather than engage in collective action, such as unions, the waitresses' forms of resistance were often unconsciously implemented. This applied especially to the ways in which they constructed notions of the self in spite of dominant assumptions of waitresses as passive and powerless. Resistance was enacted through linguistic conventions (narrative strategies), through which self-perceptions and understandings were enacted and affirmed. That these types of resistance have been ignored when resistance is understood as public (male), results from the gendered nature of agency, power and thus resistance.

According to Allen Feldman (1991:5), 'political agency is manifold and formed by a mosaic of subject positions that can be both discontinuous and contradictory'. Because power is decentralized and plural, so in turn are forms of political struggle. This understanding of power is attractive because, as Nancy Fraser (1989) suggests, it widens the arena within which people confront and seek to change their lives. Creating multiple stories of gender and the subject, Sarah Westphal (1994:161) posits that,

> thinking in terms of fragments means thinking in terms of choice and accountability within a vast range of possibilities, which enables the feminist thinker to sustain ambivalence in the face of inherently conflicted situations, rather than resorting to premature closure.

Maintaining ambivalence and ambiguity become powerful ways to disrupt and thus create spaces for the unimaginable. Rather than focus on how discourses invent subjects, Deborah Britzman (1995) focuses on the negative space, that which is unarticulated, unspoken and unimagined. This is the space that makes possible the mapping of a subject. In this case, 'resistance is not outside of the subject of knowledge or the knowledge of subjects, but rather as constitutive of knowledge and its subjects' (Britzman 1995:154). To envisage resistance at the microlevel of society, in which identity is always in formation within the nexus of power relations, suggests that experiences of domination and subordination are 'effects' of power rather than as proceeding from a specific course of power. How does this reconceptualization of the subject prompt new ways to theorize gender as a construct central to feminist theorizing?

Feminist theory without gender

The decentred subject, like all discourse, is contradictory. In one specific moment it could result in a political relativism and paralysis, thus undermining the project of feminism. In another, it could increase the sites of potential subversion and provide new ways to imagine concepts like agency and resistance. While the apolitical tendency of poststructuralism is disturbing to many feminists, I would maintain that it is precisely the loss of the unitary subject that is necessary for a political revisioning of resistance and agency. The fragmentation of the subject provides new ways to reconceive gender and to reimagine concepts like the subject that are central to theorizing feminism. The dichotomy of a 'unitary self' as a product of Enlightenment thought (the irony being that this unitary self is a fiction created through postmodern discourse) and a 'non-unitary' self (which ironically becomes the true self) is, as Jane Flax (1990:210) points out, itself 'partially determined by the absence of any systematic consideration of gender or gender relations'.

The deconstruction of the subject has required feminist theorists to reconsider the very foundations of their social theorizing. This decentring of the subject necessitates the eradication of 'gender' as a binary model of domination proposed by earlier feminist theories in which gender was theorized as either a complex network of identity formations produced in power relations or as an ideological system in which patriarchy required difference in order to assert male dominance (Braidotti 1994). The subversion of patriarchy is, according to Wittig (1983), predicated on the abandonment of the whole gender system, including the category of woman. Gender, the category until recently central to feminist theorizing, has become increasingly unreliable and suspicious (Nicholson 1994). Judith Butler (1990) speculates as to the usefulness of the category of gender since feminist deconstruction solidifies the very category that it seeks to problematize.[20] Teresa de Lauretis (1987) attempts to avoid the dualistic positioning of theories of gender as grounded either in power relations or ideology by suggesting what she calls a 'technology of gender'. Female identity construction is both material and symbolic. Gender is a complex technology that functions to regulate normative male and female identities.

Engaging various theories by 'doubling up' or 'tripling up' is paramount to acknowledging the specificity of gender relations. This specificity is perhaps our best claim against essentializing as a totalizing narrative. Simultaneously, engaging 'essentialism' (i.e. dominant discourses) can be useful to feminist politics at particular moments because it reminds us that a political theory must attend to the local, historical and cultural context of power relations.[21] The rejection of universal categories that theorize gender, oppression and other social relations has been done in the name of acknowledging difference and diversity. Yet, I concur with Jane Roland Martin's (1994:639) recent warning about the 'dangerous traps' of eschewing essentialism. She states that 'I can think of no better way to dampen the creative spirit or to reduce interpretive diversity than to draw up a list of concepts to be avoided at all costs'. By banning essentialism or sameness from our repertoire of methodological constructs we limit the very plurality that has been central to feminist theorizing. To reproduce 'absolutes' through banning any talk of 'essentialism' is to potentially reproduce the very essentialism many feminists have sought to deconstruct. The irony of this trap, when interrogated from the perspective of gender (thus an essentialist argument), is that the political immobilization caused by the fear of accusations of essentialism actually serves the interests of patriarchy.[22] To reject *carte blanche* that women have any commonalities in the name of privileging difference is not only to 'cut us off' (Martin 1994:646) from any political groundwork as feminists, but also to construct other women as 'utterly Other' (p.646).

What, then, becomes of feminist theorizing when gender is in 'trouble'? I maintain that we still do not know what gender is, or whether it can be a useful category for thinking about social relations. Yet as I embarked on my research with women teachers it seemed *essential* that I set aside my preconceived notions of gender, especially because the social construction of the woman teacher has been central to the regulation and maintenance of normative female gender identity. I had to resist traditional notions of resistance because in many ways these functioned to construct and maintain male gender identity. How gender was continually in a state of production and never stable or fixed forced me to view gender and resistance in a new light.

Resisting resistance: women teachers and the politics of identity

Attention to the specific contexts of power relations provides a site from which to take seriously the lives of women teachers. Within the lived experiences of women teachers as they negotiate the complex and contradictory discourses of gender and education, we not only see how theory works, but also how we can continue to theorize. How, then, do teaching and poststructural notions of resistance intersect? Valerie Walkerdine (1990:3) maintains that 'teachers are not unitary subjects uniquely positioned but are produced as a nexus of subjectivities in relations of power which are constantly shifting, rendering them at one moment powerful and at another powerless'. For Walkerdine, resistance is not just struggle against the oppression of a static power; relations of power and resistance are continually shifting. This focus on the social practices that constitute everyday life is, as Foucault (1980) suggests, more fundamental than belief systems when it comes to understanding the hold power has on us. That these social practices are gendered Foucault neglects. Turning to the lives of women teachers to explore the micropractices of resistance, I suspended the notions of agency as dependent on a unitary subject, resistance as oppositional and power as a possession.

Seeking the positions in the 'politics of everyday life' from which women teachers construct and are constructed, we can attend not only to the forms of resistance women enact but also to how these forms of resistance reveal historically changing relations of power. Abu-Lughod (1990) suggests the question we need to ask is not 'what is resistance?', but how does resistance make tangible the locations of power and dominant relations? How does a richer understanding of resistance help us to envisage the site of women's everyday 'fighting out'?

How women teachers 'struggle to write the moving and multiple feminine subjects against the stereotyped woman' (Wexler 1987:96) attunes us not only to the sites of conflicting gender norms inscribed in teaching, and thus the 'micropractices' (Foucault 1980) of power and resistance, but also lets us see how these stereotypes function as a form of gender regulation. What becomes essential to rethinking resistance is a focus on the 'politics of the everyday', in which certain discursive practices are refused or 'taken-up' and new ones created. How women teachers negotiate the tensions between dominant stereotypes of women's nature and social role and the meanings they give to their work is central not only to rethinking resistance but fundamental to rethinking pedagogy and curriculum from women's standpoints.

Notes

1 The debate as to what constitutes fiction and what constitutes theory raises the issue of how knowledge is legitimatized and how ways of knowing are validated.

2 Reproduction theory, most notably articulated in *Schooling in Capitalist America* by Bowles and Gintis (1976), attributed the reproductive role of schooling in maintaining a capitalist society to a 'correspondence principle', in which schools function to mirror and reproduce a stratified class structure and dominant social practices.

3 Larabee (1992) points out that these educational reforms, with their focus on an expert 'knowledge base' not accessible to the average lay person, is not only a salient example of Foucault's knowledge–power relationship, but functions more to raise the status of university teacher educators than bring about reforms to the teaching profession.

4 Part of the crisis in education in the mid 1980s as articulated by Bloom (1987) and Hirsch (1988) was the lack of a common knowledge base shared by all Americans. This 'lack' threatened to undermine American cultural unity and lead to Balkanization. In effect, these criticisms functioned as a backlash to multiculturalism.

5 Pinar's argument draws on psychoanalytic theory to examine how power relations and their analysis are always gendered. The reproduction–resistance binary is symbolic of the father–son Oedipal struggle. The son (and here Pinar is referring to Marxists and neo-Marxists) possessed by the need to control reproduction, in other words, to determine origins, becomes the father, and 'resistance' functions to perpetuate dominant relations rather than rewrite them. Marxism and neo-Marxist theory thus does little to shift actual power relations but instead reconstitutes them.

6 As Cocks (1989:64) suggests in her discussion of the notions of power and resistance of Gramsci, Williams, Said and Foucault, their criticism of macrostructures as dominative power is based on the fact that there are always experiences to which 'fixed forms' do not speak, aspects of actual consciousness diverging from 'official consciousness'. The existence of experience not entirely vanquished by dominating systems is, after all, how we know they are dominating.

7 Female student resistance to gender norms and expectations of femininity are the focus of several recent studies including Adams (1994), Lesko (1988) and Roman (1988). The work of Angela McRobbie (1982) has been central to maintaining that gender, as well as class, is a significant category for understanding agency among female adolescents.

8 The liberal discourse of reason has been particularly problematic for feminists who see it as central to women's oppression. Particularly important for feminists (Keller 1985; Hawkesworth 1989) has been the establishment that 'reason' does not exist independent of the self. For if this were the case, then bodily, historical and social experiences would not affect reason's structure. In effect, women's experiences would continue to be delegitimized and relegated to the world of the 'other', or as deviant. 'Reason', Mary Daly (1973:9) suggests, has served as 'a kind of gang rape of women's minds'.

9 Other studies on resistance highlighted the shortcomings of resistance theory as conceived by Willis and others in the 1970s. Bullough *et al.* (1984) suggest that

resistance theory has been overly simplified and confused with opposition to authority. They argue that resistance can develop only when there is a conscious intention to bring about change. Similarly, Weiler (1988) warns against the potential of any act of opposition being labelled as resistance without considering the quality of that resistance. Ethnographic studies by Connell *et al.* (1982) and Simon (1983) suggest that an understanding of resistance, as opposed to deviancy, can be achieved only by looking at the broader context within which schools exist. They are critical of the decontextualized, abstract nature of many studies, which neglect the interaction of family, school and work in the constitution of subjectivity.

10 Bordo (1993) is particularly critical of the credit given to Foucault for the reconceptualization of the body as a medium of social control. In *Feminism, Foucault and the Politics of the Body* she traces the rightful parentage of the 'politics of the body' from Wollstonecraft through Marcuse and Dworkin. Sawicki (1991) also suggests that the ongoing work of women of colour, lesbian women and Third World women to problematize universal categories of 'women' has been central to the critique of universal theories and the disruption of unitary, static identities. That the work of feminists and Third World peoples is obscured in the postmodern turn is the irony of postmodernism and cause for caution for many feminists who see postmodern theory as a neo-conservative philosophy and guise under which white, male, Western thought emerges again as a hegemonic discourse.

11 Harding (1987) suggests that relativism is fundamentally a sexist response that attempts to preserve the legitimacy of androcentric claims in the face of contrary evidence.

12 Feminists grappling with the tension between postmodernism and feminism with the most compelling arguments are those who also situate the dilemma within the larger structures of power relations of a postcapitalist, late twentieth-century society (Spivak 1987; Alcoff 1989; Flax 1989; Fraser and Nicholson 1990; Lather, 1991).

13 Not only have women been excluded from or marginalized from the centres of power, but because women have not set the ground rules for social existence they have not been able to name what constitutes power, resistance or social change. For women, the position from which they experience power is fundamentally different from that of men. First they have been excluded from shaping dominant social relations and their naming. Second, the very notion of experience as the legitimate indicator of what is right or wrong with the world, or even what the world is like, can be called into question by men since being a woman in a patriarchal society means being someone whose experience of the world is systematically discounted as trivial or irrelevant (Leck 1987).

14 Bartky (1990) points out that when power is everywhere, power conceived in so diffuse a fashion loses its role in an effective political critique.

15 The Anita Hill hearings are a lingering reminder of this reality (see Morrison 1992). The real–political–material consequences of the loss of the 'unitary subject' woman for feminists is a serious consideration within these theoretical debates.

16 Cain (1993) provides two powerful examples of how women's experiences have been 'real' despite the fact that these experiences were not expressed in discourse;

sexual harassment was an unconsidered relationship until feminist theorists named this form of oppression. Thus the experiences of women took place without a discourse in which to name them. These types of nondiscursive experience signify not only the phallocentric nature of language but necessitate thinking about experience and identity formation for women as in part shaped by repressed or subjected knowledges, in other words experiences that defy representation. It is this form of experience that might entail the use of imagination and intuition as a means of subverting discourse, necessitating a radical rethinking of issues of power, agency and resistance.

17　This argument is not limited to feminist critics. Altieri (1994:109) drawing on Wittgenstein's notion of 'asymmetrical logic' also asks the question 'how do we speak about what we cannot imagine representing in any adequate way?'

18　As Sawicki (1991:7) points out, Foucault does not completely reject identity based politics, but rather the search for a 'true' identity as a basis for universal emancipation.

19　As Nietzsche (1956) suggests, the legitimation of sites of power as self-evident needs to be interrogated for fictive elements.

20　Nicholson (1994) also suggests that gender as a useful category is suspect. The traditional distinction between sex as biology and gender as cultural in effect reproduces a binary in which the concept of 'gender' is dependent on the concept of 'sex', thus in effect, solidifying and making real an essentialist category. This results in a conception of gender as an additive, or 'coatrack', view to biology.

21　P. Smith (1988) points out that the current deconstruction of the subject does not necessitate the total abandonment of essentialism. He draws on Spivak's claim that we need to take the 'risk of essence' in order to increase the substantive efficacy of feminist resistance.

22　As Martin (1994:650) also points out, the rejection of essentialism functions as 'the prime idiom of intellectual terrorism and the privileged instrument of political orthodoxy'. She points out the double standard in some feminists forgiving male theorists (Michel, Jacques and Jean-Francois) for their essentialism due to their inattention to women, but taking a punitive approach towards women, in particular Carol Gilligan, whose work is rejected as having no redeeming qualities due to its essentialism.

2 Agnes: 'It is not what you teach, but who you are'

A sprig of early spring greenery – a bewildered student – or the chaos of our present world situation these things she views with an eye for the beauty, good and wisdom contained in them.

A sincere interest in *You* as a person is uppermost in her human contacts, and the limits of her time and energies are boundless as she offers an encouraging hand, a counseling work, or a sympathetic ear to all students – especially those so many miles from home.

A true teacher, a model of goodness and sincerity, but more than that – a friend.

(National College of Education yearbook, 1954,
Dedication to Miss Agnes Adams)

When I arrived at the nursing home on a stormy April afternoon in 1991, it was clear that although using a cane, Agnes was still agile and very spirited. At 94 years old, Agnes was the oldest of the life historians interviewed. Having just finished reading Ronald Reagan's autobiography, her 112th book since living in the nursing home, she proudly shared with me a log of all the books she had read, which listed the titles as well as a brief description. *Newsweek*, the *Christian Science Monitor* and the latest issue of *Elementary School Teacher* lay in a pile on the coffee table. Obviously, Agnes was still as sharp, curious and interested in world events as I had been told. While discussing my research interests with me, a family friend from Chicago began telling me about Agnes Adams.[1] Although I was primarily interested in collecting the life histories of secondary social studies teachers, I listened to how Agnes had started her teaching career in a one-room school on the Kansas Prairie in 1915, graduated from the University of Chicago in 1924, received her Masters degree in 1930 from Columbia's Teachers College, taught early childhood education at the National College of Education for 41 years and then married for the first time on her retirement at 68 years old. Despite the fact that she did not fit the profile of the 'life historians' I was seeking I realized I could not pass up the opportunity to interview her. It seemed I had no choice. Also, at 94 years old, there wasn't much time left.

At the outset of this research I could not have anticipated the connections I found between women's educational history and the life history of Agnes Adams. Little did I know that I would be able to trace Agnes's 41-year career at the National College of Education to a larger network of women reformers and activists, including those at Hull House, where Agnes had supervised student teachers at the Mary Crane nursery school during the 1930s and 1940s.[2] The Mary Crane nursery was part of a long history of collaboration between the National College of Education and Hull House as well as an expansive network of women educator activists, including Jane Addams, who saw early childhood education as central to the goals of progressive reform.[3] Although Agnes was one generation removed from this group of progressive urban reformers, she worked with Dr Alice Temple (her major professor at the University of Chicago), Elizabeth Harrison (founder of the Chicago Kindergarten College) and Edna Dean Baker (Harrison's successor as President of the National College of Education from 1925–49), all of whom had been contemporaries and colleagues of Jane Addams. These women shared a belief that kindergarten education was central to the progressive agenda. Although representing a wide range of philosophical viewpoints, these women were united in the belief that women should be central to forming public culture.

In choosing to go to Chicago, Agnes entered a city with a rich history in education. Alice Putnam, Anna Byran and Elizabeth Harrison were at the forefront of a movement 'destined to revolutionize the world' (Harrison 1890). This revolution – the education of the child – was at the centre of the women's agenda for progressive reform. Women activists throughout the 1870s and later had successfully drawn on the dominant ideologies of women's separate sphere to argue for women's role in social housekeeping. For middle-class and upper middle-class women the rhetoric of feminine altruism and motherly charity was embraced as the cloak under which even the most forceful social and political actions were advanced (Ryan 1979).

At the time of the first interview I scarcely realized that the work of early childhood educators, in particular the kindergarteners, had been central to the work of social reform, and to redefining gender. For women activists, education, and in particular early childhood education, provided a crucial space from which to actively shape understandings of childhood, mothering and teaching. The agency of these women educators seemed obscured by the dominant discourses of teaching as women's true profession and the stereotypes of women entering teaching solely because of a sentimentalized 'love of children' or 'natural duty'. Little did I realize that these women were part of a larger network of women activists and social reformers, who saw education as central to social reform.

After our first interview, I realized that Agnes's story provided an unparalleled window, or perhaps kaleidoscope, into the educational past. Her story traversed the discourses of education through the twentieth century from 'women's true profession', through 'progressivism' and 'professionalization', to 'scientific efficiency'. Her narrative brought the gendered nature of these discourses into relief. How she constructed her subjectivity within these discourses reflected her continual struggle to define and redefine gender norms and expectations. In particular, Agnes's story provides a view of the ways in which changing gender ideologies were experienced by an individual as well as how the changing ideologies of education were central to shaping and defining gender.

'I didn't think of teaching at all': disrupting 'women's true profession'

According to Patricia Carter (1992:127), throughout the late-nineteenth and twentieth centuries, teaching represented the one true and honourable vocation for women, serving as the 'one exception granted to the rather rigid social belief that paid labour degraded women and corrupted their moral character'. Teaching, seen as a natural extension of women's nurturing capacities was considered to be 'women's true profession'. Despite this assumption, Agnes's narrative suggests that she was in two minds about her decision to enter teaching.

> At first, I didn't think of teaching at all and then I had two aunts who were teachers and an uncle who was a professor so it was rather natural that I should get into teaching. Girls in our community rarely went into anything but teaching. I can't think of them going into anything but teaching.

Agnes's juxtaposition of her characterization of teaching as 'natural' and that 'girls rarely went into anything else', and her own recounting that 'I didn't think of teaching at all' suggest Agnes's conflicting understandings of self in relation to social norms and expectations. In claiming that she 'didn't think of teaching at all' she suggests that she was immune from the 'natural' roles prescribed for women. It was also difficult for me to believe that Agnes had not thought of teaching at all when in fact several close family members were teachers. Her father's two sisters (Aunts Sue and Joyce) were teachers, as was his older brother, who was a professor of English at Cornell. According to Agnes, her mother had also taught for a year in Florida before marrying in October 1892.

Positioning herself outside these dominant ideologies, Agnes takes up a counter-hegemonic position in relation to the gender norms. At the same time, her portrayal of teaching as natural, thus invoking dominant gender ideologies of teaching as 'women's true profession', allowed her to resolve conflicting feelings regarding her decision to teach. By 'taking up' the discourse of teaching as women's true profession she creates the conditions in which she can justify her decision to become a teacher. Still, her narrative allows her to construct her decision to enter teaching not as merely complying with dominant ideologies but as an active subject writing her own story. Agnes simultaneously resists and appropriates hegemonic gender discourses. Her appropriation of dominant ideologies thus becomes not acquiescence but a form of resistance.

I was struck by Agnes's telling of the tale that teaching was the only profession open to women, when clerical and nursing professions were also possible. The fictive element in Agnes's narrative comes into relief when juxtaposed to the story of Christie Devon, the protagonist in Louisa May Alcott's 1873 book, *Work: A Story of Experience*. Although the story of Christie takes place several generations before Agnes's story, it provides a glimpse of the choices women had if they became independent working women. At the outset of Christie's work life, she brazenly declares that she would not teach because she did not wish to 'wear [her]self out in a district school for the mean sum they give a woman' (Alcott 1873:13). Instead, her story chronicles the occupational choices open to white, native-born, single women: domestic servant; actress; governess; companion; seamstress; home textile worker; housekeeper; secretary to a minister; and nurse and cook during the Civil War. Teaching was not the only profession open to women. By the time Agnes entered the workforce in 1915, the choices for women seeking respectable employment had expanded to include clerical work, stenography and nursing, as well as other professions. In fact, several previously male occupations had by this time emerged as dominantly female professions, in part due to the active work of women to create more opportunities in the workforce, particularly in what had been male middle-class occupations (Fine 1990).[4] The fact that Agnes said that teaching was the only profession open to women suggested to me the conflict that Agnes experienced by taking up a profession that was deeply gendered as women's work, and thus devalued.[5] How she negotiated the conflict of taking up an identity as teacher, a subject position in which she lacks authority and value, with her own self-understanding as powerful and value-worthy, reveals the dynamic of power relations.

Her decision to teach was strongly influenced by her father through his confidence in her and his death when Agnes was 18 years old. She remembered her father very fondly.

My father's feeling that I could achieve anything I attempted gave me confidence. I was much closer to my father than my mother. Mother would always ask me my point of view, and she knew that I'd always have the same as my father. I would always do anything to be with my father. I helped him with the milking, would go out gardening with him, anything I could do. Anything to be with him. When my father died, I helped my mother raise the younger children, so I had to help support the family.

Unfortunately, William died suddenly in 1915. That same year, Agnes began teaching in the one-room school in Reno County, Kansas. One tragedy was followed by another when the following year, Herbert, Agnes's older brother drowned while on duty for the National Guard. Agnes recalled,

> Mother lost her husband in April of 1915, her mother in October of 1915 and her first born, Herbert, in July of 1916 – leaving myself, Marshall, Mary and Martha on the Kansas farm. Marshall quit school and took care of the farm. We rented the farm and moved to Emporia so we could all be together in better schools.

In 1915, at 18 years old, Agnes, now the oldest child, was responsible for her mother, 15-year-old Marshall, 12-year-old Mary Joyce and 8-year-old Martha Sue. Like other young women of the time, Agnes was not alone in having to find work as a means of helping to support her mother and siblings. It was at this point that she turned to teaching. From 1915 to 1917 she taught in a rural school where she 'had 27 children, 5 to 16 years, with 42 classes a day in a one-room school'. She recalled her experiences as a one-room schoolteacher.

> The Bell School, a one-room affair in Central Kansas, was the scene of my first teaching. My father had died the spring previous to my high school graduation, so I lived at home and drove Barney and my new buggy the five miles to school. Here, after caring for my horse, I served as custodian, caring for the cleaning, fires, first aid and attempting to teach all subjects. Twenty-seven children, ranging in age from twin 5-year-olds to a postgraduate of 16, who was only two years my junior, made up my class.
>
> Going back to my year at Bell School, during the two coldest winter months I stayed at the Vera Lee Home (Vera Lee was clerk of the board) and took Opal to school. This eased things a bit, saving two hours a day of driving time. Mr Lee said he never saw a teacher work so hard in preparation.
>
> It was a long school day, especially for the 5-year-olds. We went from 9 o'clock to 4 o'clock with an hour recess at noon and two 15-minute recesses in the midmorning and mid-afternoon for toileting and maybe a game or two. The daily programme consisted of opening exercises, fifteen to twenty minutes in which we had to salute the flag, sing around the organ, and then share interesting experiences or read a book or story. Then came classes – several with only one, some with four or five children. While these were going on, other children worked at their seats, following assignments on the board or preparing for upcoming classes.

Despite the sentimentalized visions of the independent schoolteachers that Agnes's narrative evoked in me, her recollections were much more ambivalent.

> Our school building had double desks, varying in size enough to seat the children comfortably. I allowed the children to choose their own desks, which brought on a difficult situation for the Burlings, who were 'sewed up for the winter', so some children seated nearby complained of the odours. Thinking of a solution, we played 'Fruit Basket Upset', asking all to change seats. At noon of the second day, as we dismissed for noon recess, who should be at the front door but Mr. Burling, a large horse, black snake in hand, inquiring why I had changed the seats of his children! I explained that all had changed. What might have happened then I cannot imagine, for providentially one of the board was passing by and evidently sensed trouble, so intervened.

My romantic illusions of one-room schools are shaken as I imagine Mr Burling at the door, smelling worse than his children, with mud caked on his woollen trousers, and a scruffy beard, towering over 19-year-old Agnes with whip in hand. Despite the rhetoric of teaching as women's true profession, I am reminded that the control of the profession remained in the hands of male administrators, school board members and, in this case, male parents. Teachers' behaviour at the turn of the century was strictly regulated, and this control extended to their private lives. Women teachers were not to marry and could not smoke or drink, be seen in a carriage with a man or be out after 8 o'clock in the evening.

For Agnes this control and regulation must have conflicted with her own self-understanding as a competent and creative teacher – one who managed to teach 42 classes each day across eight grades, and was teacher, basketball coach and caretaker. She claimed that 'had I not gone to a rural school myself, I'd never have survived'. For Agnes, teaching was hard work; there was nothing 'natural' about it. How she negotiated her own experiences of teaching with the dominant ideology of teaching as 'natural', and thus easy, and the increasing regulation and control of teaching as it was becoming a female dominated profession is nowhere more apparent than in the discourse of the 'rural school problem'.

'I had to learn to teach': the defeminization of rural schools

> Fortunately, one-room schools have disappeared, but there are some good things to be said for them, though it is at best a very difficult position.

Despite my romantic visions of the independent schoolteacher teaching in the one-room school, Agnes recognized the 'difficult position' women teachers faced, not only in terms of the vulnerability of women and the resultant control and regulation, but also in terms of the sheer workload.

With 42 classes a day and an hour at noon and morning and afternoon recesses of 15 minutes, you can see class periods had to be very short. Children had to become very independent since the teacher had to be busy with so many classes. But children at their desks learned much from listening to older children as they recited.

The teacher had to be on the playground during recesses to play games with the children or supervise their games. One year we had a basketball team that sometimes played with other schools. I'd never played basketball so I had to learn fast, to become referee. When there was accidents or illnesses, a child was dispatched to a nearby neighbour's where there was a phone, to summon the family to take the patient home or the teacher had to give first aid and/or phone the doctor and wait for him to come several miles. For there was no nurse on hand.

Each evening I had to stay up late to prepare lessons and materials for the next day – to work ninth-grade math problems so I could help my smart ninth-graders, or plan the history lesson carefully so I'd keep generals on the right side. We had no work books. First-graders did have a box of letters with which they'd spell out the spelling words or answer questions the teacher put on the board. The teacher wrote directions on the board to save time. Sometimes the young children would read and receive help from the older children but you see children usually had to work without help from the teacher since she didn't have time to help individuals so it was *very* hard for both teacher and children.

We always had what we called opening exercises in the morning. The teacher often read a continuing story at this time. This not only gave the group a common, unifying experience, but it set a good example for reading. Then we saluted the flag and had music. I'd have groups gather round the organ as I played and all sang.

Ironically, it was those aspects of the one-room rural school – the peer teaching, the sense of community, the independence children derived from the multi-age experience, the individualized instruction – highlighted by Agnes that were being criticized by educational 'reformers' as the 'rural school problem' (Tyack 1974). These reformers argued that a 'community-dominated and essentially provincial form of education could no longer equip youth to deal with the changed demands of agriculture itself or with the complex nature of citizenship in a technological, urban society' (Tyack 1974:14). In other words, rural schools needed to adopt the blueprint of urban schools in which consolidation, efficiency and bureaucratization guaranteed the order necessary for modern, industrial life. This order required characteristic features of the one-room school to be abolished, including nongraded primary education, instruction of younger children by older children, flexible scheduling and a lack of bureaucratic managers between teachers and community. A shift in the locus of power was afoot, in which the community was usurped from its position of control by the professional educator.

In 1914, the year before Agnes began teaching, Ellwood Cubberly (1914:105–6) wrote,

> Because the rural school is today in a state of arrested development, burdened by educational traditions, lacking in effective supervision, controlled largely by rural people, who too often do not realize either their own needs or the possibilities of rural education, and taught by teachers who, generally speaking, have but little comprehension of the rural-life problem . . . the task of reorganizing and redirecting rural education is difficult, and will necessarily be slow.

Certainly, rural schools were plagued with such problems as inadequate buildings and equipment, discipline problems, irregular school attendance, a 'bookish' curriculum and community interference or warring. However, the movement to centralization was part of a larger movement to defeminize teaching by making it more 'professional'. What often remains obscured in traditional accounts of the 'rural school problem' is the gendered nature of the discourse of school reform. That the majority of rural schoolteachers were women (87.6 per cent in 1914) made them vulnerable to attack. According to Suzanne Clark (1990), the rural woman schoolteacher at the turn of the century came to represent the preindustrial, the pastoral and thus the backward, agrarian and untamed. The increasing polarization of urban and rural schooling was solidified in part through a gendered discourse, in which urban signified modern, industrial, expert, professional, public and thus male whereas rural signified country, agrarian, community centred, sentimental, private and thus female. Progress in the eyes of many school reformers necessitated the transformation of these rural schools along an industrial model. This 'narrative of progress' (Clark 1990) necessitated the separation of schools from what was traditionally associated with the female, and their relocation in the public domain; that associated with the male. The gendered nature of school reform discourse was so successful in establishing the ideology of professionalism that the facts of the successes of one-room schools were neglected. Agnes's own state, Kansas, which was wholly dependent on the country school system, in fact had the highest literacy rates in the country in 1900.[6]

The power of this discourse on the 'rural school problem' was evident in Agnes's own narrative. After four years teaching in rural, one-room schools, Agnes decided to leave Kansas to attend the University of Chicago's School of Education.[7] When I asked why she left teaching to go back to school she responded adamantly, 'Well, I had to learn how to teach'. Her statement reflects the changing ideologies suggesting that women's 'natural instincts' were not sufficient to the task of 'training' young children. The belief that science and psychology, as advanced in the child study movement led by G. Stanley Hall, would identify specific stages of child development and learning required insights based on the new psychology, which demanded sophisticated skills and knowledge (Weber 1969). According to Harriet Cuffaro (1991:68–9) 'the theory of evolution challenged long established truths and beliefs, and the scientific method of investigation provided a new lens for viewing children's development'. Yet, I wondered how Agnes reconciled the conflicting and contradictory ideologies that promoted teaching as women's true profession due to their 'natural capacities', and the simultaneous 'deskilling' of women inherent in the discourse of scientific efficiency, which suggested that women teachers needed training to teach.

Her decision to go to the University of Chicago to 'learn how to teach' suggests that despite her own experience and expertise as a teacher she believed she needed professional training. That one-room schools were seen as backward, could have contributed to a 'rhetorical victimization' (Clark 1990) in which women teachers allied themselves with professionalization and the discourses of scientific efficiency, thereby participating in the delegitimation of their own knowledge and expertise. Of course, this left female teachers in a double bind of having to take up a male subject position (i.e. expert, professional) while simultaneously being warned that they might lose their femininity (i.e. spinster) if they joined the public, working world of men. Agnes's narrative is an example of the deft negotiation of these conflicting gender ideologies embedded in teachers' work. In maintaining that teaching required training and was a 'profession', with a set of skills that could be learned, teaching shifts from 'women's work' (private/female), and thus devalued, into the public realm (male). Her claim that she needed to learn how to teach undermines the essentialized discourse of teaching as women's true profession, and in claiming that teaching had to be learned the 'naturalness' of the gendered nature of teaching is disrupted.

In recounting her decision to attend university in order to 'learn to teach' Agnes's narrative clearly reflects the shifting ideologies from essentialized notions of teaching as women's true profession to scientific notions of teaching as a profession. For Agnes, these ideologies worked to shape understandings of her gendered identity in complex ways. Her belief that she had to 'learn how to teach' reflects the emergence of scientific efficiency as manifested in the 'rural school problem'. She appropriates this ideology, which in essence undermines her own experience and expertise as a teacher, and two things happen. First, Agnes can justify her decision to attend the university. Second, by claiming that teaching requires a knowledge base she disrupts the essentializing discourse of teaching as women's true profession. Consequently, these ideologies are taken up in ways that both reproduce and resist gender norms.

The discourses of teaching as women's true profession and scientific efficiency were also intricately linked to shaping and being shaped by the larger gender ideologies of the 'new woman'. Specifically, Agnes's narratives highlight how she negotiated understandings of self within the conflicting gender discourses of separate spheres that had supported the notion of teaching as women's true profession and the newly emerging gender discourses of equality and the 'new woman', which supported notions of professionalization. An understanding of male and female as distinctly different and complimentary to an understanding of male and female as equal was a radical shift in gender ideology. The changing image of teachers in cultural representations was central and integral to this shift. Agnes's story highlights how educational discourses of professionalization and progressivism in fact worked in complex ways to construct new gender ideologies as well as reposition women in traditional gendered roles as facilitators of knowledge.

'Woman adrift'?: The new woman and teaching

Agnes's decision to move to Chicago in 1922, although becoming more commonplace as young women had more professional and educational opportunities, must still have been a daunting one for 25-year-old Agnes. Her decision to leave her family to move to an urban area was, however, part of a growing trend of 'women adrift' that had begun as early as the 1880s, in which 'more and more women began to live apart from their families and to make it in a burgeoning, nonagricultural, urban labor market' (Meyerowitz 1988:xv).[8] Especially on smaller farms daughters were the first to leave home. A national study of the farm population in 1920 by the US Census Bureau reported 'the farmer's daughter is more likely to leave the farm and go to the city than is the farmer's son' (quoted in Meyerowitz 1988:9).

And yet, leaving behind her mother and younger brother and sisters could not have been an easy decision considering the expectations for daughters to take care of widowed mothers and younger siblings. Yet I believe that the fact that Agnes had a well established aunt in Chicago, her desire to further her education and the potential financial rewards must have influenced her decision. In 1924 the average annual salary for elementary schoolteachers in Chicago was $2387 (Fine 1990). Despite the higher cost of living, and considering her salary of $230 a year in Kansas, Agnes would most certainly have been able to increase her financial contributions to the family. Her decision to attend college, specifically at the University of Chicago, was probably based on the fact that as a young unmarried woman she would need a guardian. Her father's sister, Aunt Joyce, a high-school teacher in Chicago, provided Agnes with a suitable place to board. Agnes believed that her aunt, who had been a close friend of John Dewey, played a major role in shaping who she was.

The aunt with who[m] I lived during my years at the University of Chicago and my early college teaching was really a second mother to me – she had wide interests, liberal viewpoints and deep interests with those around her and I find myself reflecting these qualities in my own life, since I lost both parents at a relatively young age.

Agnes was not, much to my surprise, unusual in her decision to attend the university. Although in 1890 there were only 3000 female college graduates, by 1900 females accounted for 40 per cent of the graduates of American institutions of higher learning (Ryan 1979). In 1920 this figure was 47 per cent. Interestingly this figured dropped substantially by 1950 to only 30 per cent. By 1920, 5 per cent of the nation's doctors, 1.4 per cent of the lawyers and judges, and 30 per cent of the college presidents, professors and instructors were women (Ryan 1979:141). Leadership of the progressive women's organizations was drawn from the largest generation of single and childless women in American history (Ryan 1979). Overall, 75 per cent of female professionals were single in 1920.

In part, Agnes's decision not to marry reflected the emerging image of the 'new woman' as independent and autonomous. Simultaneously, Agnes reminded me that on one level the fact that she hadn't married was the result of the regulation of women teachers. She recalled, 'For many years, the day a girl got married she was taken off the roll. She stopped teaching. Principals didn't feel that she could carry on two careers.'[9] And yet, in pursuing why she hadn't married she also recalled,

> I have had people ask me many times, 'Why didn't you marry?' And of course when I was overseas they just expect that everybody is married. But I would say to them, I didn't have to. 'What do you mean you didn't have to?' Well, I was taking care of myself financially and so I didn't have to marry because of financial reasons . . . I think teachers should be dedicated and involved. That of course is one the things that bothers me today. When women have a couple of vocations, when they are married and have homes and families, it's hard for them to take in so many of these other activities. There are not too many of our faculty who still belong to the AAUW [American Association of University Women]. I'm always so glad when they do, because it's good for us as teachers to have contacts with other people in other fields.

Agnes's decision not to marry and have children reflected her commitment to a set of values in which women educators were redefining what constituted a vocation (traditionally only motherhood) as well as what constituted family: 'I had so many children in these contacts through school, living with young women and helping them solve their problems, that I had a family'. In redefining family as a larger network of connections, Agnes contests the dominant gender norms of the nuclear family, in which women were restricted to the private sphere and dependent on men financially.

Contrary to the dominant belief that women entering teaching have a low commitment to work and enter teaching only as a stopgap until marriage, Agnes made a conscious decision not to marry and instead devoted herself to the education of teachers. She was not alone. In choosing a life course in which she rejected the 'marriage plot', she was supported by other women who advocated a special role for women (Scott 1993). She was part of a larger community of women educator activists, including her closest mentors, who remained single and carved out alternative lifestyles that rejected the nuclear family.[10] All three of her mentors, Elizabeth Harrison, Alice Temple and Edna Dean Baker had chosen not to marry and had committed their lives to promoting early childhood education.

Agnes recalled that although Alice Temple did not marry she did have a life-long companion.

> Miss Martin and Miss Temple lived together and they were as different as people could be. Miss Temple was a very restrained and rather austere person. I knew another side of her as we went to one of the national conventions at ACE [Association of Childhood Education] and that she had so much more fun about her than I knew earlier.

Olga Adams, a classmate of Agnes's, who was devoted to both Miss Temple and Miss Martin, wrote, 'Katharine came to Chicago to prepare for kindergarten teaching and was to become Miss Temple's star student and a life-long, intimate friend. She lived in the Temple home for the last twenty years of her life and died in 1931' (Snyder 1972:200).

Like Alice, Agnes chose to live with other women. Although Agnes was not involved in an intimate relationship, she defined her relationships with the women she lived with as family.

> Aunt Sue and [Aunt] Joyce had lived in Chicago, Aunt Sue giving up her teaching and Aunt Joyce teaching in Madill (??) High School, Chicago. After Aunt Sue's death on 30 June 1919, several friends in turn lived with Aunt Joyce. Jennie Worral and her mother had lived with the sisters, then after 'Miss Jennie' lost her mother and brother she came to live with Aunt Joyce in early 1922 and in October 1922, I joined them on 3014 Jackson Blvd. apartment – entering the University of Chicago until graduation in August 1924. The following summer, so we could continue together we moved from the Jackson street apartment, a westside apartment where things were rapidly deteriorating. Since the college [National] moved to their new building in Evanston in February of 1926, we moved to 1514 Jonquil Terrace, Chicago, where we had a large apartment, situated where we all three had good transportation. When Aunt Joyce went to Boulder to help care for Uncle James, 'Miss

Jennie' and I moved into a spacious four-room third-floor apartment at 7706 North Paulina, Chicago, a block from the Howard 'L' [elevated railway] station – most convenient for transportation and fine grocery stores. By this time 'Miss Jennie' had retired from her position as a proofreader down town, and she and I made the home, with her as my homemaker until her death, 11 June 1964, nearly 96! I remained alone in the apartment until I retired from National College of Education in August of 1965 and took a position for two years in Southern Illinois University in Carbondale, Illinois.

Agnes's decision to stay single was by no means 'unusual'. When I asked if she had been unusual in choosing not to marry, she said,

No. Not in my time period. But, of course today would be very different, I mean most teachers are married and they'd never think of being disqualified because they were married. I think that marriage ought to bring an enrichment that could be used well in schools.

In not getting married Agnes joined other women educators committed to social change. Since the turn of the century women had successfully carved a sphere of influence that enabled then to experiment with alternative lifestyles based on a woman's culture that challenged the normative nuclear family. The establishment of women's colleges (like the National College of Education), settlement houses, voluntary organizations and even the promotion of early childhood education, which disrupted traditional notions of motherhood, were all challenges to the normative nuclear family. These 'women adrift' contributed to the creation of a subculture in American cities that contributed to the redefining the traditional gender roles, in which family life had defined American womanhood. As independent wage earners, living apart from family, relatives or employers, these women skirted normative expectations of traditional domesticity in which women's lives were defined within family life. In many ways the work of the early childhood educators can be seen not as compliance with traditional notions of women's 'natural' love of children but as a means to reshape public culture in ways that incorporated and valued women's knowledge.

Although middle- and upper-class women forged new definitions of gender, they differed from the emerging group of wage earning women who were economically dependent on themselves.[11] Agnes falls somewhere between these two groups. Not dependent on a low wage job, Agnes was also not materially privileged and certainly would not have been considered upper middle class. She supported herself financially although she lived with female relatives and companions until she married in 1968. Agnes provides a picture of womanhood at the nexus of the shifting gender ideologies. Her narrative must be understood within these changing ideologies of women as having distinct and separate roles and the 'new woman'. According to Kathleen Weiler (in press: 26), this ideology of the new woman was characterized by an 'emphasis on equality and the acceptance of a gender-neutral ideology of professionalism'.

Although Agnes was obviously committed to promoting the role of women in shaping and rewriting public culture, this was not done without conflict. Taking up the role of the 'new woman' was plagued with contradictions. Although this image suggested an independent woman, becoming too independent implied that one had become defeminized. This negotiation between being the 'new woman' (in many ways a male subject position) and maintaining one's female subjectivity was reflected in Agnes's recollections of Edna Dean Baker.

> Miss Baker focused so completely on education. She was a rare soul. She was a very frail person, but she thought like a man. She made decisions with background and she was very feminine but, as I say, she thought as a man when she worked with these leaders of various fields. She had broad vision.

Despite by then having been popularized, the image of the 'new woman', which was characterized by modern individualism, contained conflicting messages about the self-seeking woman. On the one hand, the independent woman characterized the American ethos of individualism, hard work and progress. Simultaneously, this new woman, popularized in fiction and film through the cultural icon of the 'flapper' was portrayed as sexually promiscuous. As Kathleen Weiler (in press: 32) maintains, 'the impact of the constructs of the new woman and the flapper and later Freudian ideas of female sexuality influenced the ways in which women teachers were viewed . . . The image of the unmarried teacher subtly shifted as she became perceived as a sexual or deviant threat'. Agnes's decision not to marry was now seen as abnormal because it did not conform to the emerging heterosexist ideology, which maintained that healthy women were to derive their sense of self through, and in, marriage. Single women teachers who did not comply with these emerging gender norms of heterosexual behaviour were characterized as 'spinsters'.

The spinster is represented as the sexless, unwomanly, unmarried creature, whose image embodies the consequences of women's refusal to comply with and be the subject of men's social and sexual power. When heterosexuality is one of the ways in which men's power over women is maintained, the spinster or lesbian functions as a threat to that power.[12] As Jill Conway (1971) suggests, this sexually neutral type is often identified with the professional expert or the scientist, as compared to the woman sage (mother–teacher), who relied on women's special nature for knowledge. The irony is that women are valued for their natural commitment and ability to work with children, but sanctioned when they place this work above patriarchal expectations and gender norms that require dependence on men. For

women teachers positioned within the intersections of these conflicting ideologies of teaching as 'women's true profession', based in the ideology of
separate spheres, and the 'professional' teacher, based in the ideology of the
'new woman', this requires a deft negotiation of gender subjectivity. Thus
Agnes struggled to construct a notion of gendered identity in which one
could 'think like a man' (be a professional) and 'be feminine'. In continually
shifting between these ideologies she disrupts the power of these discourses
to work in hegemonic ways. Consequently, unitary, essentialized gender
norms are rejected. How Agnes negotiated these conflicting gender norms
and ideologies in terms of the meanings she gave to teaching is what I now
turn to. These gender ideologies took on specific meanings within discourses
like 'progressivism', 'professionalism' and 'scientific efficiency'; discourses
that were central to shaping Agnes's life, beginning with her decision to enter
the University of Chicago in 1921 to study early childhood education.

Disrupting 'super vision'

On 29 August 1924 Agnes Adams marched in the University of Chicago
convocation procession to the music of Wagner's *Die Meistersinger*. Sev-
enty-three candidates for the degree of Bachelor of Philosophy in Education
were presented to Dean William Scott Gray. Agnes was also one of nine education students to be awarded honours in excellence from all the university
departments of the senior colleges (only 43 awards were given). After graduation Agnes began working at the National College of Education's Student
Teaching and Placement Office. At the time, the college was an all-women
school located on the south side of Chicago. Her interest was in working
with student teachers through supervision. The college had an opening and
Dr Alice Temple, her professor, recommended her to the Dean, Miss Edna
Dean Baker. Despite many other offers she chose the National College of
Education and stayed for 41 years.

Agnes's belief in the progressive ideals of education, the primary role of
women in shaping education and society, and the context of a well established women's culture was in severe contrast to the realities of schooling in
the mid-1920s, in which 'social efficiency' was the norm of the day. This was
particularly the case in Chicago. In 1923, the Chicago Federation of Labor
(CFL) denounced attempts to organize the city's schools on a factory model
(Wrigley 1982). According to the CFL, the goal of the school board was to
pour children into the hopper at one end and grind them out at the other end
'as perfect parts of an industrial machine, calculated to work automatically,
smoothly and continuously for a short period' (Wrigley 1982:1). During the
1920s the conflicts over the curriculum and scope of education of working-
class children centred on issues such as the use of IQ tests, the introduction
of the junior high school and the development of tracking systems (Wrigley

1982:48). The CFL argued that the children of workers should receive a broad liberal education. They specifically opposed tracking, in which working-class students would be restricted to a vocational education. Labor consistently supported more child-centred teaching, increased taxation to support schools and the teaching of a wide range of subjects (Wrigley 1982).[13]

Within this contest to define education, the field of supervision emerged as an outgrowth of the bureaucratization and social efficiency movement, which maintained that teaching could be reduced to a set of skills that could be measured. In taking up the role of supervisor, Agnes took part in the 'professionalization' of the field. In other words one interpretation of her choice could be that she was complicit in the discourse of scientific efficiency. Simultaneously, Agnes's education at the University of Chicago, although weighted heavily in technocratic views of education, was steeped in progressivism as well. Agnes considered herself to be a child-centred, progressive educator.

Traditionally within feminist and critical theory, progressivism is seen as a liberatory discourse in education, whereas technocratic views of education are seen as oppressive.[14] I would maintain that discourses of progressivism and scientific efficiency both work simultaneously as liberatory and oppressive. And both are implicated in and central to regulating normative gender identities. Valerie Walkerdine (1990:19) has argued that the

> liberation of children conceived in progressive terms did not mean the liberation of women. In some ways, it actually served to keep women firmly entrenched as carers. Women teachers became caught, trapped inside a concept of nurturance which held them responsible for the freeing of each little individual, and therefore for the management of an idealist dream, an impossible fiction.

She questions here the concept of liberation as freedom from overt coercion. As Michel Foucault (1980) suggests, 'liberation opens up new relationships of power, which have to be controlled by practices of liberty'. In the case of 'progressive' teachers, they were to allow the individual to unfold and grow according to their own needs by providing maternal nurturance.

What became evident to me in Agnes's narrative was that while conceiving the purposes of education very differently, both progressivism and social efficiency were predicated on the assumption that women's influence on education should be indirect. In the case of progressivism, women's agency was to be subjugated to the child, and in the case of social efficiency it was to be subjugated to the 'expert' or 'principal'. In the following section of this chapter I attend to how Agnes negotiated the gendered nature of these discourses as she simultaneously took up the role of 'expert' in her position as a supervisor as well as taking up the role of 'facilitator'. How Agnes takes up these identities, and when, provide a window into how she negotiated her gendered subjectivity. The discourses of progressivism and social efficiency are neither inherently liberatory nor oppressive, but are and continue to be sites through which we are gendered in complex and contradictory ways.

Entering the University of Chicago signified, in part, Agnes's decision to align herself with the modern university as opposed to the normal school university (teacher training). By the time Agnes arrived at the University of Chicago, the debates over the nature of progressive education had been submerged by a comprehensive curriculum revision and the definition of a new, scientific approach to pedagogy.[15] Perhaps no one manifested this vision more than Charles Hubbard Judd, Head of the Department of Education, who exemplified the new manager; he was 'the perfector of the message of a science of education'.[16] For Judd, the teacher was a worker. Agnes was to take directions from an administrator who would have been apprised of the principles of efficient education by researchers at institutions of higher learning.

Thus, by 1923 the educational currents had shifted such that the progressive legacy of Dewey was considered by many as outmoded and imprecise. By the early 1920s the focus of teacher training had begun to shift from a cohesive liberal curriculum to specialized courses on the methodology of teaching. By 1922, the number of special education courses had increased from 3 to 13, courses in teaching and research from 5 to 25, and those in educational administration from 5 to 26. In fact, by 1931 teacher training was considered to be at the periphery of the primary mission of the School of Education, the College of Education was disbanded and all teacher training programmes were transferred to the control of academic departments within the university.

In 1923, Agnes entered the College of Education, one of four institutions comprising the School of Education, the other three being the Graduate Department of Education, the University High School and the University Elementary School. The fundamental purpose of the School of Education was to,

> organize education on a scientific basis and to equip students with a knowledge of the principles of educational psychology, school organization, and methods, and to give them a survey of the historical development of educational institutions so that they will be prepared to carry on educational work independently and scientifically.
>
> University of Chicago, *Annual Register* 1922–3:400

Although it is unclear whether Agnes took courses in the graduate department, the description of the nature of the courses certainly reflected in general the tenor of attitudes regarding teaching and education in which,

> the idea which has controlled the Department of Education from the beginning of its history is that scientific facts about school practices and

results, secured through the use of historical, statistical, and experimental methods, can be put into a form which is as specific and exact as the professional information given in schools of medicine or engineering

University of Chicago, *Annual Register* 1922–3:402

For Agnes, the University of Chicago certainly presented a site from which she could 'learn to teach' based on the most scientific methods.

Within the College of Education, Agnes entered the department of kindergarten–primary education, one of ten departments in the college with the goal of receiving the degree of PhB. The primary aim of this department was to train teachers and supervisors who would work in elementary school, high schools, colleges and universities and for which ordinary academic departments did not provide any training. As a student of Alice Temple (1871–1946), who had been Dewey's student at the University of Chicago, Agnes was introduced to the pragmatic philosophy and functional psychology that had replaced the rigid adherence of Froebelianism among progressive early childhood educators.[17]

Fundamental questions thus beset the early childhood education community in regard to the conflicting ideologies of Froebelianism, progressivism and scientific efficiency. According to Cuffaro (1991:69) educators grappled with complex issues. Was growth to be defined as the unfolding and awakening of the essential nature of the child, or was growth the realization of potential and capacity resulting from interaction with the environment? Was play to be free or directed? Was it sparked by a search for universal principles or the interests and curiosity of the child? These questions shaped the exchanges, innovations and experiments within the Chicago community of educators at the turn of the century. This was the community that Alice Temple not only participated in but also helped shape. It was the community of thought that Agnes was to inherit as well as reshape.

Agnes considered herself an educator deeply influenced by progressive ideology and, specifically, by Alice Temple, who has been considered to have been a major force in projecting the Dewey philosophy into the education of young children (Snyder 1972). It was said of Alice Temple that she 'always revealed herself and her private myth most tellingly in what she created. She and her work are one and inseparable' (Snyder 1972:191).[18] In working with Alice Temple, Agnes was to become a part of a network of women kindergarteners who saw their work as central to social reform.[19]

Working with Alice Temple as her major advisor and mentor, Agnes was, I believe, guided to pursue training in supervision (this is what she was hired for at the National College of Education on graduation). Dr Temple offered three courses relating to supervision: Kindergarten–Primary Supervision; Kindergarten–Primary Supervision: constructive criticism; and Kindergarten–Primary Supervision: general problems. In addition she offered courses in the training of kindergarten–primary teachers, problems in curriculum-making, and the kindergarten–primary curriculum.

In her final terms, Agnes did her supervision practice with Marjorie Hardy in the first grade at the University of Chicago laboratory school.[20] She recalled that Marjorie Hardy was a wonderful teacher; 'she had a deep respect for children and I certainly got that from her'. In supervising teachers she recalled that Hardy's focus was on, 'their relationship with children first. Their enjoyment of children and their understanding of children. That's what I always look for in supervision. Their relationships'. On the role of measurement in supervision, Agnes said, 'well, that isn't a measurable thing'. She assured me that they did develop checklists; in fact very good checklists. Agnes brought her students from the National College of Education to the laboratory school, but commented that, 'I was much disappointed because it seemed to be completely individualized rather than group experience'. Although Agnes had become the supervisor or 'expert', her comment revealed her rejection of the technocratic ideology on which the role of the supervisor was based. In maintaining a focus on relationships and suggesting that teaching is not a 'measurable thing', she resists the dominant ideology of scientific efficiency.

In asking Agnes to describe her kindergarten and the philosophy behind it, she replied,

> Children need to learn to get along with each other. They also need to be engaged in making decisions. In the kindergartens I worked in, we had a doll corner, we had clay, and sang and played and so on, but it wasn't an academic thing. Now, kindergartens are so often ABCs, and that isn't what children need at that age. Some children learn to read at that age and some don't, but to force all children to read is a mistake.

Her emphasis on a child-centred, experiential curriculum that focused on the emerging needs of children clearly echoed progressive ideology. But Agnes's enactment of this child-centred ideology took a rather bizarre twist. As a supervisor, Agnes was required to participate in the monitoring of these ideologies. She was caught in the ironic space of regulating young women teachers to conform to a pedagogical ideology that has as its basis the freeing of the child. This bizarre twist highlights the convergence of two seemingly incompatible ideologies: progessivism and technical rationalism.

Agnes's negotiation of these conflicting discourses and their related gender expectations was revealed in a statement in which she reflected on what she liked most about her career,

> I think [it is] the close contact with individuals. As a supervisor, I was able to visit their classrooms and see how they could best help children grow. I also had contact with children continually when I worked with the supervision in the schools. This very close contact with individuals

is very important. I enjoyed the content of the work I was teaching, but I enjoyed the individuals more. I think one important thing in teaching is that it's so much more of who you are than what you teach.

In contrast to her earlier claim that she needed to 'learn how to teach', Agnes suggests that it is 'who you are' and not what you teach. Rather than see this as a contradiction needing to be resolved, I see this as a site of gender conflict that Agnes negotiates. Two interventions take place here. One, Agnes conceptualizes supervision as teaching. In renaming supervision as teaching, Agnes subverts the hierarchy embedded in technocratic models of supervision in which the supervisor is positioned above the teacher – as having 'super vision'.[21] This displacement resituates her in a cultural space more closely aligned with female values. Second, she goes on to suggest that it is not 'what you teach', but 'who you are'. In denouncing 'what you teach' as unimportant she undermines the dominant technocratic view of learning and supervision in which the expert passes on knowledge. In claiming that 'who you are' is important she reclaims a relational dimension to teaching that values the agency of the individual. Her narrative strategy of repositioning suggests a site where Agnes is grappling with conflicting gender expectations.

Taking up the roles of supervisor and expert was a form of compliance with the ideology of professionalism and scientific efficiency. Yet by her redefinition of that role, Agnes subverts the ideologies even as she embodies them. By simultaneously subverting and embodying these ideologies she resists prescribed gender norms for women. What this highlights is the ways in which representations of these discourses as oppositional obscures the ways in which both progressivism and social efficiency regulated gender norms.

Reflections

I continue to be simultaneously lured by the complexity of Agnes's life and the illusion that I will somehow be able to solve the puzzle of fitting her life into neat little categories. I struggle to make sense of her life, and yet at the same time, I recognize that the harder I try, the further removed I get. In writing her story I have become more aware that the writing of a life history is not about 'getting the story right'. I can never recapture Agnes's life.[22] I can, however, interpret the complex ways in which she negotiated her life as a form of self-representational agency. The contradictions Agnes's life embodies are in themselves a strategy for displacing dominant gender ideologies. Agnes's story disrupts traditional notions of power and resistance to gender norms by showing how the simultaneous appropriation and rejection of gendered subject positions posited by dominant ideologies subverts their power. This subversion suggests one way in which Agnes contests any unitary tale of resistance.

Notes

1 I am deeply indebted to Audrey Holtan for sharing her knowledge of Agnes Adams with me. See also Meyer (1989).
2 The National College of Education is now the National Louis University in Evanston, Illinois. The college, originally known as the Chicago Kindergarten College, was founded by Elizabeth Harrison as an all women's college in 1893. Harrison, who had studied with Alice Putnam (an avid promoter of the kindergarten movement in Chicago, especially within the settlement house movement) in 1879–80, was at the forefront of advocating training for all women who would work with children (mothers, teachers and nurses). The college grew out of the Chicago Kindergarten and Training School established in 1887, in which the primary goal of training classes for mothers was to convert their aimless actions into an intelligent plan. As Beatty (1990) maintains, kindergartens' work with mothers can be viewed as an attempt to raise mothering to the status of a vocation.
3 As early as 1888 the Chicago Kindergarten and Training School, later to be renamed the National College of Education, worked across class lines with several settlement houses, such as Hull House, Chicago University Settlement and The Commons, where students did their student teaching.
4 According to Fine's (1990) study of female clerical workers in Chicago, in terms of the hours, wages and conditions of work, a clerical position was one of the best occupational opportunities for women at that time.
5 Apple's (1985) analysis suggests that there is a relatively strong relationship between the entry of women into an occupation and the slow transformation of the job as less skilled and valued.
6 As Clark (1990) points out, it was precisely the characteristics of one-room schools that were being criticized, that have been attributed to the success in educational achievement of these rural schools including help children received from each other, younger children getting help from older ones, allowing each child to progress at their own rate, and the lack of competition and the personal attention each child received. In fact, the one-room school, with its diversity of students, mirrors the now desirable mainstream classroom. The management systems of rural schoolteachers seem to have been invisible to the experts, according to Clark.
7 Agnes had already earned a life certificate at the Kansas State Normal School, where she studied from 1917 to 1919. She returned to teaching for 1919–21.
8 From 1880 to 1930, the female labour force increased from 2.6 million to 10.8 million (Meyerowitz 1988). In Chicago, the female labour force increased from 35,600 in 1880 to 407,600 in 1930, an increase of over 1000 per cent. By 1930, one-quarter of all adult women and over half of all single adult women worked in the waged labour force (Meyerowitz 1988:5).
9 According to K. Weiler (in press), in 1928, the National Education Association surveyed school systems in 1532 cities with a population of more than 2500; 29

per cent of these cities still required that teachers who married resign at once and 25 per cent more forced them to resign at the end of the year.

10 Central to Agnes's work were her networks, both formal and informal, of women educators. Women historians (Cook 1977; Cott 1977; Prentice and Theobold 1991) suggest that personal friendships and relationships provide essential support systems for politically active women. For women who often define themselves in terms of their connections with others (Belenky *et al.* 1986), these relationships not only sustain them but suggest the establishment of communities that are pivotal to developing collective investment in social change. This relational understanding of change, in which power is decentralized and dispersed, posits alternative epistemological frameworks from which women teachers constitute acts of agency.

11 See Showalter (1978), Rosenberg (1982) and Smith-Rosenberg (1985).

12 See Oram (1989) and Khayatt (1992).

13 Wrigley's primary thesis is that despite revisionist historians' (Tyack) claim that the hegemony of an elite imposed schooling on the working class, she posits that the working class was continuously involved in shaping the discourses of public education. In this same vein, I will argue that middle-class women were a significant force in shaping educational discourses.

14 See Munro (in press a) for a further elaboration of how these discourses are gendered in complex and contradictory ways. Also see Marshall (1995).

15 Taken from the *Guide to the College of Education Records 1900–1926*, The University of Chicago Library, Department of Special Collections, The Joseph Regenstein Library, 1980.

16 From an interview with William Pattison, former Dean of Graduate Studies, 20 July 1992, University of Chicago.

17 According to Cuffaro (1991), at the turn of the century the aims and practices of the field of early childhood education were in profound conflict. The idealism of Froebelianism, with its inherent belief in the natural unfolding of the child was in contrast to the emerging pragmatic philosophy and functional psychology, which replaced the notion of the absolute with a naturalistic conception of 'life activity' as the basis for an epistemological standpoint (Westbrook 1991:71). William James, a fellow pragmatist, described this shift as an empiricism in which the ' "life" of "experience" is the fundamental conception and there is nothing real, whether being or relation between being, which is not direct matter of experience' – an objective process of interacting variables undergoing constant 'reconstruction' (James (1898) taken from Westbrook 1991:77). Rather than a mere unfolding of natural processes, humans were engaged in a continual process of meaning making. The rejection of an absolute idealism and the role that education played in fostering not a predetermined set of principles or body of knowledge but a continual reflection of experience was the challenge taken up by Chicago educators and reformers.

18 Alice, a native of Chicago, attended the Chicago Free Kindergarten Association in 1889, where she studied with Anna Byran, someone Alice always thought of as 'a pioneer in progressive kindergarten education' (Snyder 1972:190). She eventually worked as a critic teacher for Anna Byran at the Chicago Free Kindergarten Association and succeeded her as Principal after her death in February 1901, where she remained until her resignation in 1904 to study at the University

of Chicago. As a teacher at the Free Kindergarten Association and associate of Anna Byran, Alice joined a group of radical kindergarten teachers who were at the forefront of not merely criticizing Froebelian orthodoxy, but of reconceptualizing the very definitions of early childhood education. See Parker and Temple (1925).

19 This group, not a cohesive one, included a diverse set of individuals including John Dewey, Jane Addams, Anna Byran, Alice Temple, Elizabeth Harrison, Alice Putnam and Ella Flagg Young, who engaged, through their interactions in the kindergarten movement, in debating, theorizing and implementing the implications of this radical shift in the relationship between the individual and society. See Munro (1995; in press)

20 Marjorie and Agnes eventually attended Teachers College, Columbia University together and lived across from each other in the dormitory. Marjorie did not return to Chicago but went to Philadelphia, where she headed the Germantown Friends School.

21 The intersection of supervision and curriculum has been a contested field in which the role of supervision as an application of curriculum or integral to theorizing curriculum has been debated. The critique of supervision as a neutral site for the implementation of curriculum has been discussed by Bowers and Flinders (1990). For supervision as a gendered and cultured discourse see Jipson *et al.* (1995).

22 The story presented here is incomplete. Agnes's participation in shaping the field of early childhood education was a life-long endeavour. During our first interview she spoke of her attendance at the American Association of University Women (AAUW), at 94 years old, in terms of her most recent involvement in the education profession. In fact, Agnes was involved in a wide range of professional networks including: Delta Kappa Gamma; The National Association for Childhood Education, in which she served as vice president from 1942 to 1944, and in 1948 served as a member of the advisory board of the Chicago branch; The Association for Curriculum Development and Supervision; the Association of Childhood Education; and she was a charter member of the AAUW at the National College of Education. Her work at the National College of Education also included establishing international exchanges with Korea (where she taught on several occasions) and maintaining and shaping the college's relationship with Hull House's Mary Crane nursery.

3 Cleo:
'I could have lived another life and been just as happy'

I tended not to follow the norms . . . what I'm thinking of right now is that Atlanta was made up of many cultures. As a young girl I went to school downtown. I had [the] bus fare but we would walk. It was two, three miles. My friends and I would go out and spend the money we saved on ice-cream or something. Anyway, in that walking we went through several residential areas, the Jewish part, the Italian section . . . I made friends in those culture groups. I never had any close friends who were blacks except who worked in our homes. We always had black servants. I had a Jewish friend. It bothered my mother and my sister for me to go to her home, my sister more than my mother, and I didn't understand that. Then I had a friend from junior high who was Greek, and she would come to our home. And, I don't remember her home but I know I was there, but it bothered my folks and I guess the more it bothered them, the more I did it. I don't know, but I tended to pick friends from groups who were not smiled on by my parents.

I remember the big discovery for me in Atlanta, about Mill Town. I knew there was a Mill Town. I knew there were mills, but I had no personal experience with them. And, then I had a friend who had relatives who lived in Mill Town. I went there with this friend one day and had the shock of my life. Junior high maybe. Here was this huge wall. And I knew that wall was in Atlanta, around a certain section. Mill Town was in that wall. Inside. I never had known what was on the other side of that wall. And inside were factories and company homes. I don't think I was ever there maybe twice at most with her. But, that was a real revelation. I didn't know there were people like that. The company ran your life. They worked within that wall. They lived within that wall. Their lives were inside that wall. And, I can remember how shocked I was.

As Mary Catherine Bateson (1989) suggests, story telling is fundamental to the human search for meaning. In trying to make sense of my life as a teacher, my search for meaning and understanding is linked with the stories of other women. By hearing their tales, I begin to understand mine. As I listened to Cleo tell this particular story I was flooded with memories of my own childhood friends and the experiences that had awakened me to the worlds outside my upper-middle-class upbringing. The realization of just how small my world was prompted me to resolve that I would never be trapped by its walls.

Cleo begins her story, 'I tended not to follow the norms'. She positions herself outside normative conventions. She is not like those whose lives were 'inside that wall' – who worked within that wall, lived within that wall and whose lives were run by the company. Her memory of a 'huge' wall, no doubt a symbolic construction, suggests the profound nature of her realization of the social constraints and restrictions imposed on 'others'. The 'shock' that Cleo receives signifies, I believe, her own emergent understanding as a female adolescent of how walls or 'norms' circumscribed her own life as a result of gender, race and class expectations. Her construction of a 'huge' wall, her remembrance of this, is important precisely because it reveals more than factually accurate accounts. As Alessandro Portelli (1993:12) maintains, 'the importance of oral testimony may often lie not in its adherence to facts but rather in its divergence from them, where imagination, symbolism, desire break in'. For Cleo, the wall symbolizes not only the gender and racial norms, roles and institutions that constrain women's behaviour, but also her agency in defying these norms by breaking with class and racial social conventions.

It is no coincidence that Cleo begins her story with a 'rebellion or counter-narrative'. The importance of this narrative strategy in women's lives is, according to the Personal Narratives Group (1989), the site that it provides for women to contrast self-image and experiences with dominant cultural models. Her narrative of adolescent 'awakening' is a compelling story, which positioned her as a strong, determined female rebel–heroine who resisted dominant gender expectations by 'not following the norms'. As Passerini (1989) suggests, the self-image of the born rebel can be of great help in transforming reality. And yet, her self-representation as a rebel, although compelling, seemed to mask the conflicts unavoidable for women who struggle against gender norms. While the masking of conflicts resulted in Cleo feeling empowered, and provided me, the feminist interpreter, with what I thought was resistance and agency, the irony is that both these positions threatened to erase female subjectivity by reproducing masculinist discourses and humanist assumptions of the self.[1] In essence, her self-representation as a rebel functions simultaneously to reproduce dominant gender norms and contest them. Consequently, I saw Cleo's narrative of rebellion less as a 'true' self-representation, but as a site where Cleo struggled actively to construct a gendered subjectivity.[2] In this site of negotiation we can attend to the complex and contradictory ways in which we construct a gendered subjectivity. With a growing understanding of this tension, I turn to Cleo's stories of her family relations, a pivotal site from which she constructed and negotiated a gendered subjectivity.[3]

'Certain things you do: certain things you don't do'

Cleo's tendency towards rebelliousness or her anti-authority stance became clear to me on several levels in our early interviews. When I asked her age, she flatly refused to answer. A friend, raised in the south, pointed out to me later that I had perhaps offended her, since asking a woman's age was considered inappropriate by southern standards and something one just did not do. Yet, I also considered that her refusal to tell me her age was just part of her assertive, almost stubborn, disposition, a trait she might have inherited from her maternal grandmother, the 'matriarch' of the family, who 'no one ever challenged'.

I imagine Cleo, somewhere in her sixties, to be much like her grandmother. At our first meeting it was hard for me to believe that she was retired. Her brisk walk, youthful look, and energetic manner all belied her age. She has an energy and sense of independence about her that I find uncommon in women of her generation. The central role her grandmother played in shaping Cleo's own experiences became a theme to which we would return over and over.

As Cleo described her, it seemed life centred around her grandmother.

> We just all respected her [grandmother] a lot. Both our parents and my cousins and I. We had a dynasty! She was the matriarch . . . the head of the clan. It was the southern style of living. She had the big house and when things happened to her children, we all returned to the big house. We were always together on special days. Always. There was no such thing as somebody being with the other in-laws. They were at grandma's!

For Cleo it was clear that one did not question her grandmother: 'We respected her and knew that she made the ultimate decisions on everything.' It was clear that you just did certain things, 'like wearing white gloves and a hat, even if it was just to the corner store'. In a society where public authority and power in social relations are generally the domain of men, Cleo's grandmother, like Cleo herself, seemed not to fit the 'patterns of womanhood' that prescribe that women have no authoritative place in public life (Aisenberg and Harrison 1988). Cleo and her grandmother assumed the ready-made roles and social prescriptions of womanhood that dictated 'wearing white gloves and a hat', and yet, although Cleo and her grandmother adhered to these public expectations of southern womanhood, they simultaneously subverted gender roles and expectations by taking up positions usually reserved for men

(Cleo as an administrator and her grandmother as a political force). Was femininity is this case, 'wearing white gloves and a hat', a 'masquerade' (Riviere 1985), or was it as Walkerdine (1990:143) has suggested 'a performance, a defence against the frightening possibility of stepping over the gender divide?'[4] For Cleo, the tensions between the dominant gender norms of women as passive and her lived experiences of gender in which women are active and powerful are sites of profound contradiction.

Compared to Agnes and Bonnie, Cleo's story also stands out because she does not talk about a male or paternal figure in her youth. For her the process of identification entailed not choosing between the mother and the father, but instead between the two central female figures in her life; her mother and grandmother. The strong presence of her grandmother in Cleo's childhood can be in part attributed to the early death of her father, a Methodist minister, who died when Cleo was a baby. Although she remembers little of her father, 'the family always speaks well of him . . . in spite of the fact that he was a minister, not because he was one'. With his death, Cleo, her mother and her sister Charlotte, five years her senior, moved in with her grandmother.

Despite the typical expectations for women that Cleo described as 'I think you were expected to get married and have a family', her own experience of being raised by her grandmother and mother, both of whom were economically independent, was in contrast to societal norms. Cleo clearly recognized that dominant expectations for women revolved around the 'marriage plot', but Cleo marks her confusion regarding this expectation in her statement, 'I *think* you were expected to get married and have a family'. Her own lived experiences of her mother and grandmother contested this master narrative. Her qualifier of 'I think' signifies a rupture in which Cleo contests the hegemonic power of dominant gender expectations. Cleo's narratives of her grandmother and mother suggest her ongoing negotiation of female gender identity, in which being female is not equivalent to being powerless or less highly valued. To have agency without giving up a subject position as female, which assumes powerlessness, requires complex strategies.[5] I elaborate on one of these strategies, the myth creation, as an example of Cleo's negotiation of conflicting gender expectations.

Cleo's grandmother's behind-the-scenes involvement in Atlanta politics took on a mythic nature.

> She knew the political bigwigs in Atlanta. She knew Woody [Woodrow] Wilson when he was a law partner in Atlanta. And she called him Woody. She was well connected. And she talked about it. I was so amazed when I was getting my degree in history, and I'd ask her about people and she would know them. She'd say, 'Oh, we lived next door to him'. Stuff like that, and she had nicknames for all of them. And I couldn't believe it that these were the people I studied about.

Cleo's admiration was obvious as she showed me one of two pictures she shared with me, a picture of a stately, white-haired woman and proudly says, 'That's her'.

Cleo never made clear to me the role her grandmother played in Atlanta politics. In fact, her unusually powerful position seems to be constructed in some supernatural way as Cleo explained when I asked her whether she was like her grandmother: 'A cousin once said, "I always respected her, but I never liked her". In my mental world, [I] never thought like that; it was not a relationship of like or dislike. Grandma was like God.' Although she misunderstood my question, her answer reveals the ominous presence her grandmother had. Cleo continued, 'Well, grandma was something of an enigma to all of us. She lived her life and we knew how to live around her. But we never knew anything private about her much . . . She had a life that we were not in on.'

This mythical or symbolic representation of her grandmother as powerful and elusive suggests one way in which Cleo was able to imagine alternative family structures that did not reflect dominant gender norms. As Luisa Passerini (1989:191) maintains, myths can be 'employed to mediate between traditional and new, between reality and imagination, between individual and collective'. For Cleo, the myth of her grandmother becomes a site from which she can envision women as powerful, as well as a site for her fears of women as powerful.

Cleo's description of her grandmother was, 'Well, she was involved in Atlanta politics in a way. Now she never held a job, but her friends, people that she associated with, were connected.' I asked Cleo whether that was where her interest in politics came from, and her response was, 'No. Because that was not her; it was her connections.' Her grandmother's influence came not through holding a formal government position, but as a result of informal power relations. Working outside 'the' system to manage the formal relationships of power was, initially in my estimation, her grandmother's greatest influence. Although Cleo has learned that women are not to hold power, she acknowledges that women have found ways to circumvent the cultural scripts that situate women as compliant. Knowing whether Cleo's grandmother actually had power or not, or how she obtained it if she had, is not as crucial as understanding the power of the myth that Cleo creates in order to envision women outside traditional gender norms. Her grandmother, in Cleo's mind, must have posed a threat to patriarchal relations, and thus Cleo was able to experience how a woman could negotiate being both a woman and powerful.

The complex nature of her relationship to her grandmother was revealed to me when at the end of one of our interviews Cleo commented, '[I] never questioned that all families weren't like that, with large institutions behind them'. If one agrees with Mary Bateson (1989:113) that 'family life provides the metaphors with which we think about broader ethical relations', Cleo's framing of her family relations in terms of a large institution – symbolic for her grandmother – suggests the 'naturalness' that women can and do hold power. The mythic and symbolic nature of the story of Cleo's grandmother may, as Luisa Passerini (1989:191) suggests, 'draw its power and *raison d'être* from the very fact of not being 'true', but rather from acting as a source of inspiration, encouragement, and excitement *in the face* of a different social reality'. By constructing her grandmother as overturning gender roles, while simultaneously upholding certain gender expectations, the image or myth of her grandmother is 'employed to mediate between traditional and new, between reality and imagination, between individual and collective' (Passerini 1989:191). For Cleo, this mediation is embodied in her statement that she 'doesn't try to change things, but will resist them'. Although initially, I might have interpreted this as compliance with patriarchy and lacking agency, Cleo's story suggests that the importance of her narrative is not in its representation of 'reality' but lies in recognition of the symbolic and its potential influence on forms of actual behaviour. Cleo has learned that although you do not change institutions (in particular patriarchy), this does not mean women are without agency or need to comply with dominant gender expectations.

A driven drifter

Cleo's self-representation as a rebel was particularly evident in her resistance to dominant images of women's central role as being in the private sphere. She recalled, 'Well, I never questioned it. I just always did it. I got a job when I was in high school, which was totally unheard of by both my family and in my social group. But I wanted a job.' By choosing to begin work at an early age, she separated herself from her family, rejecting their class norms. She perceives herself as being different from her family, especially from her sister, who she describes as 'never having worked; she wasn't a career person'.

While attending her first two years of college in Atlanta, Cleo worked for the city government, 'When I worked in the civil service commission, we got a request in for, I don't remember how many office workers, to Panama Canal headquarters. I was in the recruiting office, so I recruited myself and my cousin.' Cleo's mother, thinking they wanted to go to Panama City in the neighbouring state of Florida, agreed to let the girls go. After eighteen months in Panama, 'I went to Seattle. I got a job with a lumber company as a secretary and I worked the whole time I was there. I also was a reader to an English professor. I did crazy things.' I asked whether 'doing crazy things' was characteristic of her family. Her firm response, 'No. Just of me,' seems to reflect her strong desire to lead an independent life.

Cleo's early independence – leaving home at 20 years old to go to Panama, followed by her move to Seattle, where she pursued a degree in English, economics and history at the University of Washington, hoping to become a government economist – did not fit my picture of the norms for young women raised in the south in the 1930s and 1940s. These years of travel, schooling and various jobs, Cleo attributes to chance. Despite her decision to work, Cleo also describes her career as one that was not planned. 'Things just happened', was her common response to queries about the stages of her career. What seemed to me like a natural career progression from teacher through department chairperson and district social studies coordinator to regional district coordinator, was not, Cleo reflected, 'conscious. I didn't plan ahead. I was a *drifter*.' Her description of herself as a drifter contrasted strongly with my own perception of Cleo as ambitious and as actively pursuing a career in spite of the norms that assumed that women get married and have families. I saw her strong desire to work not only as an act of resistance to traditional norms and a desire to be independent, but as a form of creating and enacting her own identity.

In their book, *Women in Academe* (1988:25), Aisenberg and Harrison suggest that women's 'flight from their origins' is more than the usual (masculine) rebellion against one's parents in search of one's identity. Women's flights are often sustained or characterized by frequent moves, new starts and unfinished projects. The prevailing marriage plot excludes women's search for identity through the tradition of escaping convention. Women are to find themselves through marriage. For women, the prevailing norms work against a persona of independence and thus their flight is as much a search for new norms, as it is an escape. Thus, Cleo uses the metaphor of the drifter to envisage an escape from gender norms – to avoid becoming trapped within the 'walls' of societal conventions.

And yet, as Cleo described her work, I did not get an image of a drifter.

> There was order in my work. I kept a schedule every day that nearly killed me. Well, I was thinking about all the details. And I keep a schedule now. It doesn't matter if it gets interrupted. But I still have that schedule. It's a security blanket. You don't feel lost when you know what you're going to be doing.

I ask how it would feel to be lost, and she says, 'Well, to be here in the afternoon and not have anything to do. That's stuff that doesn't happen to me.'

The contrast between the order she describes as central to her daily life and her description of her career as 'not planned' illuminates strikingly different senses of self. Cleo clearly recognizes and conforms to the social conventions of femininity in which you 'did certain things, like wear white gloves and a hat, even if it was just to the corner store'. This narrative of deferral, as well as her self-representation as lacking agency through constructing herself as a drifter, coincide with her deep investment in a narrative of rebellion expressed in her stories of adventure, becoming educated in predominately male disciplines, and resisting social expectations. How was I to make sense of these apparently contradictory self-representations?

On one level, her rebellion narrative satisfied in me a desire to interpret her life as an example of how women can resist traditional gender roles and can construct themselves as active subjects. Her story of resistance, adventure and flight took up a masculinist narrative of separation and autonomy, which positioned her as powerful and independent. This reading fulfilled my desire to see women, particularly women teachers, as active agents. On another level, I was unsettled by my unitary reading. Although I was initially intrigued with the agency of her story, her use of a traditional masculinist narrative, as I understood it, threatened to erase her very subjectivity as female. Linda Brodkey and Michelle Fine (1991) suggest that women are attracted to discourses that promise to represent us to ourselves and others as empowered subjects. In taking up the masculinist discourse of the rebel adventurer, Cleo constructs herself as having agency. Although this reading satisfied my quest to 'find' resistance to gender norms, it resulted in a unitary reading of Cleo's subjectivity as male. By seeing her story as the traditional struggle for gender identity in which she is either male (rebel adventurer) or female (deferential drifter), I reproduced binary gender norms. This binary reading obscured the conflicting ways in which Cleo was grappling with her gendered subjectivity.

In my mind, Cleo's self-representation as a drifter suggested a lack of agency, and was in opposition to what I saw as the 'drive'; the competitiveness and success she achieved in her career. I now realize that I did not originally interpret Cleo's story of the drifter as a form of agency or resistance. My own understandings of resistance and change, which assumed that change resulted from deliberate and active resistance to the structures perpetuating oppression, seemed to get in the way. I did not see how women's ability to displace traditional gender norms through metaphors such as the drifter operated as a form of 'resistance'. In reading other works on women's lives (Aisenberg and Harrison 1988; Hancock 1989), I was surprised to find that the term 'drifter' frequently appeared. The image was used not in the negative sense, to denote aimlessness or a lack of motivation, but to describe stepping outside gender norms so that women might create their own concepts of themselves and their work.

Paradoxically, Cleo's lack of intentionality, through the naming of herself as a drifter, becomes transformed into an expression of agency. This self-image allows her to see herself outside societal norms; she deflects these and does not have to be defined by them. In this sense, she can write her own life. By resisting a stable coherent self, the metaphor of the drifter provides a continual displacement of gender, always keeping it in flux. In disrupting the binary construction of gender, 'reversing and displacing its hierarchical construction, rather than accepting it as real or self-evident or in the nature of things' (Scott 1989:92) Cleo deconstructs the scripts written for women.

Thus, for women the 'authoring of self' (Casey 1993) by re-writing patriarchal scripts is a fundamental form of resistance.

Reconceptualizing resistance as grounded in the ability to displace gender
norms through metaphors like the 'drifter', Cleo deconstructs normative
gender roles and expectations by positing subjectivity as non-unitary. This
displacement of the unitary subject becomes a form of resistance because it
allows Cleo to take up shifting and multiple positions in relation to power
dynamics. When resistance is experienced as shifting, never consolidated,
always in flux, unable to be named, power is understood as dispersed rather
than as oppositional. For women who have learned that they are not to be
powerful, this rewriting of power creates a space from which they can envision or imagine themselves as active agents. The drifter is able to disrupt, to
diffuse and take up a position from the margins from which, as bell hooks
(1990:145) suggests, women can 'envision new alternatives, oppositional
aesthetic acts'. In narrating her life, Cleo's self-representation that 'she could
have lived another life and been just as happy' is one such oppositional act.

Becoming a teacher: 'I could have lived another life and been just as happy'

Cleo began her life story by telling me, 'I could have lived another life and
been just as happy'. We met at a coffee house, perfect strangers, having
talked only once briefly on the phone. Was she telling me that she could have
been just as happy without being a teacher, knowing that teaching was the
focus of my study? I was taken aback that someone who had committed
more than thirty years of her life to teaching, administration and social
studies curriculum reform could so easily have 'lived another life'. Where
was the committed activist I sought who took up teaching as an act of social
change? This was not the resistance I was seeking. Was this the story she
thought I wanted to hear? What kind of aesthetic act was this? Why, I wondered, did she tell this particular story?

Initially, I interpreted her statement as a form of false consciousness; a sign
of her own investment in the devaluation of teaching because it is women's
work.[6] Her ambivalence towards teaching not only mirrored my own resistance to becoming a teacher, in which I saw women valorized as 'nurturers'
and consequently positioned for oppression by an essentialized discourse, but
highlighted the complex ways in which we construct our lives despite the
gender myths regarding women's supposed natural capacities. I understood
her story that she 'could have lived another life' as signalling a site of struggle
in which she negotiated conflicted gender ideologies. To take up an identity
as a teacher, a traditionally female profession (disempowered), must have
conflicted with her own self-representation as an empowered intellectual and
rebel (male, empowered). By constructing this narrative of imagination in

which 'she could have lived another a live', she asserts that she did not have to give in to the essentialized gender expectations embedded in the dominant discourse of teaching as 'women's true profession'. In retrospect, her story is consistent with her earlier self-representations as a rebel, drifter and adventurer. Rather than read the tension between her 'lived' life as a teacher and her imagination of another live as a contradiction, I see this as a 'critical vantage point' in which the negotiation of conflicting subjectivities provides a site for redefining resistance.

Because I did not understand her ambivalence to teaching as resistance at the time of the interview, I pursued my line of questioning, asking her how she started teaching. 'Probably the way people stumble into most anything. I had hoped to go into economics. But that was because I had worked in Atlanta which was a government centre and my first job was at the civil service commission.' Her response that she 'stumbled' into teaching lacked the agency apparent in her other stories. To stumble means to trip, to fall unsteadily, to blunder or to make a mistake. That is not how I defined resistance. Could it be that we were resisting our resistance to patriarchy's script for women by entering teaching as a way of coming to terms with our female subjectivity, something that we had stalwartly denied in our investments in self-representations that situated us within discourses that resonated with notions of male subjectivity: the rebel, the adventurer and the lawyer.

Despite her rebellion narrative Cleo did become a teacher. Her decision to become a teacher is even more significant in light of her family's strong disapproval. She reflected,

> No one in my family was a schoolteacher. When I first mentioned it to my family, I remember that my aunt objected strenuously. She said, 'Cleo, you don't know what you're talking about.' [What was her objection?] Well, I'm not sure actually that I even know. It just wasn't something that we did. [If it wasn't what you did, why did you do it?] A lot of my friends were doing that.

Cleo simultaneously resists what I interpreted as her family's class bias towards teaching as a middle-class profession. By claiming that all her friends were doing it, that teaching was indeed women's true profession, Cleo is in effect once again the drifter, someone being carried along by others, moving along the lines of least resistance, and being propelled by forces over which she has no control. In order to become a teacher (take up a position of female subjectivity and a different class position) Cleo must absolve herself of any agency so she does not consciously submit to the patriarchal script written for women. In effect, this deft manoeuvre in which she 'lacks agency', becoming the drifter, allows her to reconcile her decision to become a teacher without disempowering her.

Cleo's invoking of the dominant ideology of teaching as 'women's true profession' contrasted strongly with my own deeply embedded notions regarding resistance and change, in which the conscious rejection of hegemonic ideologies is central to bringing about change. From a critical and neo-Marxist conception of resistance, I initially interpreted Cleo's engaging of teaching as 'women's true profession' as giving in to the male plot, as a form of 'false consciousness'. Yet, for Cleo, invoking dominant ideologies allowed her to defer her family's disapproval and thus created the conditions in which she felt she could justify her decision to become a teacher while redefining teaching to fit her identity as teacher–intellectual. Trinh Minh-ha (1991:17) has suggested that in engaging dominant ideologies while simultaneously disrupting them, women 'narrate a displacement' as they 'relentlessly shuttle between the center (patriarchal norms) and the margins (their own understandings)'.

After college graduation, still drifting, Cleo returned to Atlanta.

> I didn't know what to do. I had done the methods course and taken the practice teaching, so I looked for a job. My mother knew so many people in the Department of Education so I thought I could go right into the Atlanta schools. But, they did not take inexperienced people. You had to have three years experience to go into the system. And, so I looked for a teaching job outside Atlanta. Jobs were being advertised, and I found one in a town that I'd never been in and I even agreed to take the job, but they insisted that I had to attend the local church and take part in community affairs on the weekends . . . Anyway, I said this is nuts, I'm not going to do that. And so I came back to the west and got a job teaching here.

Cleo returned to the Pacific Northwest and accepted a position as a high-school social studies teacher in Gilman, a working-class town of 70,000 where the economy was based on the timber industry. 'You want to tell me about your first teaching job?' I asked.

> No. Well, the conditions were very different then. Well, there was no such thing as a free period. When you took a job teaching you taught every period of the day, you had large classes. I remember in Gilman that we had forty, we were allowed a maximum of forty chairs in a room, and I had forty-two enrolled in a class . . . And I taught as many as 200 kids a day. And we did a lot of paperwork. I worked every night on papers.
>
> One night, I remember, I took my papers to a PTA meeting that I had to go to. I couldn't seem to get those papers finished. So I took them with me to work on during the out times when something else wasn't going on and I had someone strongly object to that. One of the parents said, 'If you don't have any more interest than that, why do you come?' I thought, 'Lady, you don't know what you're talking about.' I said, 'I'm not working on it now; I just wanted to have it when I had time.'

But we really worked. We worked hard. But we didn't question it. That
was the norm.

In addition to the regular teaching load, teachers were expected to participate in extracurricular activities. For Cleo, this included attending football
games, directing the school play, being in charge of the pep squad, and working on the school newspaper. 'I just laugh when people say they've got three
preparations. My land, we could have six.'

Eventually, Cleo started the Advanced Placement (AP) course in US history at Gilman High School. Scheduling problems did not permit the course
to be taught during the regular school day, so Cleo held the class in the
morning a little after seven o'clock before her regular class schedule began.
Soon other departments started to offer AP courses. Cleo says that it was her
teaching of the AP course that 'ultimately started me in the direction of curriculum'. After several years at Gilman High School, Cleo was asked to
become chair of the social studies department at Goldman High School, in
the adjacent school district. This district served a primarily white collar,
middle-class community, which included a major university.

In her new position Cleo continued to teach the AP US history classes, as
well as taking on the other responsibilities generally assumed by the chair,
which included the department budget, evaluation and course scheduling.
Cleo became recognized for her student-centred teaching style, which promoted active learning and development of reflective thinking as opposed to
the traditional textbook, lecture style common in social studies.

Her interest in bringing about a more inquiry-orientated social studies
curriculum, which relied less heavily on the typical memorization of facts
and dates, seems to have been the primary factor in her 'being asked' to be
the social studies Curriculum Coordinator of the district. Cleo made it quite
clear that she 'was asked to do it . . . I didn't apply for it'. She credits two
district administrators with 'getting me into administration'. Despite her
principal's objection, Cleo moved to the district office and began a district
wide K-12 project to redesign social studies curricula. Her deferral in
actively pursuing a position as an administrator signalled a site in which
Cleo once again negotiated conflicting gender ideologies.

'No desire to be the top Joe'

From my perspective, the tension in Cleo's life between being the rebel ('one
of the boys') and her narratives of deferral (normative female behaviour) are
nowhere more apparent than in her story of becoming an administrator.
Initially, I interpreted her move into administration as a form of agency on
two levels. First, moving into administration was an example of how women
disrupt the stereotypes of women teachers as lacking motivation and career

aspirations, what Dan Lortie (1975:99) has termed 'flat career lines'. Second, I saw her move into administration as taking on a position from which she could enact change. But what I interpreted as resistance, Cleo named something else.

In light of her successful career and what I perceived as an orderly progression from teacher through chairperson to administrator, Cleo's self-representation was one that she described as 'not planned'. My initial understanding of her move 'up the career ladder' as resistance conflicted with her assertion that she did not seek promotion to district coordinator of curriculum. Despite her obvious success by male standards, she also had a tendency to play down her active role in achieving success. Regarding her role as coordinator of curriculum, she noted, 'It was something I did; it wasn't something that I was striving to change or to move to some other plateau . . . I wasn't trying to reach the top in either teaching or administration; I had no desire to be the top Joe. I didn't apply for it [the position] I was asked.'

In my desire to locate resistance in teachers, a desire encouraged by Cleo's construction of herself as rebellious against gender norms, I initially did not hear the fragmenting of her subjectivity reflected in the above excerpt about becoming an administrator. I struggled to understand why Cleo resisted conceptualizing herself an an active agent. Had she internalized patriarchal norms so well that she was merely acting out the role as the 'dutiful and appropriately meek daughter?' (Jacobs 1992). Perhaps what was troubling me was that her story of deference positioned her as a willing 'daughter' to patriarchy's desired subservience. Did her attributing her success to others signal her conflicted feeling about leaving the classroom and betraying her supposed 'natural duty' as a teacher? Or was it, as Carolyn Heilbrun (1988) has pointed out, that women have difficulty taking credit for their accomplishments because they see them as grounded in relation to others, not as individual, autonomous accomplishments.

In essence, such acts of deference engage women in a discourse that silences their agency and which therefore thwarted my desire to find resistance. Statements about her career such as 'It wasn't conscious', 'I didn't plan ahead' and 'I was a drifter' prompted me to reread her narratives. I needed to put aside my understanding of resistance as oppositional and instead, by listening more closely to her lived experience, come to terms with the idea that Cleo could have agency and act in rebellion while simultaneously being deferential. Only in this way would I be able to acknowledge the ways that non-unitary subjectivity not only emerges out of conflicting gender norms but also helps us to negotiate them. The conflicts that Cleo negotiated are evident in the detailed stories of becoming an administrator, on which I now elaborate.

To be a woman administrator is to function in a culture in which power and authority are defined by patriarchal and masculinist norms (Biklen 1983; Lieberman 1988). More importantly, our very understandings of terms like power and authority are located in and dependent on gendered understandings in which male behaviour is constituted in opposition to female behaviour (Butler 1990). For women to be female is to not have authority. Thus, to be a female administrator is necessarily a contradiction in terms. Consequently, Cleo's story of becoming an administrator focused on how she struggled with the complex and contradictory expectations of being a woman moving into a position of authority. I now turn to her narrative of becoming an administrator.

Cleo distinguished two types of administrators: those who had 'gone up the hard line' and those who made it through by virtue of their connections.

> Well, if there was a single man teacher in the elementary school, it was assumed that at some time he would be a principal. You could have thirty women teachers and there was no assumption that they would be looking into administration. But you know this.

It is clear that Cleo understood that women were not to be administrators. Also Cleo's perception that 'men have been in administration for so long, they take it for granted that they belong there', suggests once again that it is natural for men, not women, to be administrators. Her statement 'but you know this' suggests her assumption of the common understanding that women know they are not to step into roles usually reserved for men. To do so is to enter the terrain of gender conflict.

How does Cleo negotiate an identity as an administrator if the rules of the game weren't meant for women? In our discussion of the hard line, going through the proper channels, I had assumed that Cleo had gone up the hard line because of her seemingly critical stance towards coaches who had taken the easy way up through taking advantage of personal contacts. Cleo does not include herself among the people who had to take the hard line to get into administration. She comments proudly, 'I didn't do any of that; I was just giving general impressions of what people traditionally did to get into administration; men were good to me.'

I ask how she is different; how she made it. Her response is, 'I'm not different. I just sort of fell into it.' Again, I am puzzled by her perception of her career as 'just happening' and I push to find some clue by asking her to describe the stages of progression in her career.

> [Can you?] Not really. I had a lot of drive and I don't know where I got it. My mother was a very busy person, but I don't remember her having what I call drive. I always had to have a goal to do something. And I was not content when I didn't have one. And when I retired, then that goal began to be the next trip. Or some project that I was doing. Like needlework. Right now I'm going to paint this place.

I understand 'drive' to be ambition, but I sense that Cleo means personal power. Her 'drive' is something that she does not control; it is innate, unable to be manipulated, captured or tamed. I think back to her earlier statement about 'the two men who got me into administration'; her image of being 'driven' allows her to explain her success as not self-determined, but to be attributed to others, in this case the actions of the administrators. If women are not meant to succeed, although Cleo obviously does, attributing her success to other's actions or to her drive resolves or explains the disjuncture between actual life and the norms that one is expected to follow: 'It just happened' and 'I didn't have anything to do with it'.

I think that I could alternatively read Cleo's statement that she did not actively seek a promotion as a strategy for easing her conflicted feelings about taking up a position usually reserved for men. Denying that she actively sought to become an administrator allows her to maintain her identity as a teacher; a subject position less contested for women. The importance of maintaining her identity as a teacher is evident in a statement in which she adamantly names herself a teacher. 'I'm still with teacher groups. I am not with administrators. I'm with the same group of women as when we started and most of us were teaching. Now we're all retired. But they're all teachers. Classroom teachers.' Thus, Cleo's ambivalence about 'moving up' the career ladder into administration could also be seen as a way to disrupt traditional male norms that devalue teaching (female) and prize administration (male). In effect her ambivalence challenges the traditional patriarchal tales of natural and desired ascendancy to positions of power.

Biklen (1983) describes something similar in her ethnographic work with women teachers. She explains that for many women teachers moving 'up' into administration is seen as diminishing the quality of their work as educators, rather than advancing it, because they become distanced from the classroom. The decision to stay in the classroom reflects a set of values that resonates more closely with the values of female selfhood than does the decision to accept an administrative position. It also functions to avoid the potential erasure of female subjectivity when one takes up the male-defined position of administrator. Consequently, Cleo's early rebellions, her deferral of her success to others, and her investment in the discourse of teaching rather than administration not only highlight sites of conflicted subjectivity but also suggest how non-unitary subjectivity is of vital importance in women's lives for resisting gender norms. Equally critical, Cleo's story demonstrates that subjectivity does become conflicted when one has experiences that challenge received views of what it means to be gendered in this culture and in a particular profession.

I understand this to mean that Cleo made her way up into administration just like one of the boys, through her connections, because she was well liked. 'It was she and all men', she says with pride. I sense the tension between the pride she feels at having learned their game and her criticism of it for being too soft. I wonder how women teachers, who often negotiate multiple worlds with multiple sets of rules, resolve the tension between negotiating the system, and compromising their own values.

Ironically, despite Cleo's tacit knowledge that women do not become administrators, she was adamant in her belief that being a woman didn't make a difference. In other words, she did not believe that women were discriminated against. In describing her working relationships with men, Cleo did not seem to feel that being a woman made a difference. 'Well, I worked with more men than I did women. I never felt, well there were some who weren't happy, but it's because they were being stirred out of their natural rut. And that they didn't like. I don't think it would have mattered whether that was men or women on that.' I asked her what enabled her to work with men. 'I think one thing was that I always worked with a group. I never pretended to be the only one there who had the answers. But I think this kind of thing you'd probably get better from people that I worked with.'

I wonder if working in a group and diffusing her position of authority becomes a strategy for working with men, whom Cleo later describes as being more comfortable with other men, because, 'They [men] respect men more than they do women. That may not be true, but it seems that way.' Her explanation is that men are 'used to men being the authority figures', rather than women. In response to my inquiry as to whether she ever felt she had a problem with men because she was an authority figure she responded, 'Well, I can give you an example, but I don't know if I want it in your paper'.

This was not the only time Cleo asked me not to put something in my paper regarding what she considered an 'unfair' treatment. She describes her reaction to these experiences as, 'I really didn't fight it; a fight with no chance of winning is not a real good fight. You're wasting your energy to fight over that.' By not fighting the system, she does not validate it. Rather than fight the system, which Cleo had learned early on would not really change the institutions, she acquired the informal strategies necessary to negotiate the system. Ironically, one of these was deferring her own agency in becoming an administrator. In claiming that she 'had no desire to be the top Joe' she simultaneously complies with normative expectations for female behaviour of deferral and displaces the traditional male norms, which value administration (male) and devalue teaching (female). In refusing to take up an identity as an administrator, signified through her not going through the 'hard line' and in her adamant naming of herself as a teacher, Cleo is able to maintain her female subjectivity while moving into a position usually reserved for men. As a consequence, she was able to take up a position in the district as coordinator of curriculum through which she hoped to enact curricular reform. For Cleo to be an active agent of change, to have agency, presented yet another site in which Cleo negotiated her gendered subjectivity.

Moving a graveyard – curriculum change

For Cleo, the challenge of bringing about change in the teaching of social studies through reconceptualizing the curriculum became one the most exciting times of her career. Given her position, the resources and the good-will of the teachers in the district, Cleo believed she could bring about change in the teaching of social studies that would not only increase student interest, but result in their being more critical thinkers and better informed citizens.

Images of women teachers as change agents, as actively pursuing and enacting their own philosophies or beliefs about teaching, are rare. The ideological roots of teaching as women's true profession, based on their nurturant capacities, continues to constrict the image of teachers to one of primarily caretakers, in which one's own needs are subsumed to those of the students. Traditional wisdom has it that it is women's duty to carry out the ideas of educational thinkers, not to be constructors of ideas. This is not to suggest that women have not been change agents or innovators of educational thought, and it did not stop Cleo from trying to enact her beliefs about what should be a good social studies curriculum.

However, as Cleo understood intuitively, change could not be enacted by confronting a system or changing a system that was designed for men and merely tolerated independent female thinkers. As she said, 'I resisted; I didn't try to change things'. Regarding her role as change agent, she commented, 'I know that you don't change curriculum or teaching by fighting. You've got to win them [over] and they've got to respect you.' Her own experience as a teacher had taught her the degree to which teachers feel administrators are qualified to tell teachers how and what to teach. For Cleo, the most powerful method of change would be not to change the system but to resist it from the 'bottom up' by working with teachers.

The pattern of deferring her agency, or what I initially interpreted as such, was a recurrent strategy throughout Cleo's interviews. My interest in working with Cleo had been her role in social studies curricular reform.[7] As social studies curriculum coordinator in the mid-1960s she worked on a five-year project to redesign the K-12 social studies curriculum. She commented on the state of the social studies curriculum when she began the project.

> When I first visited the classes, so help me, they were teaching the Civil War the same week in the fifth grade, and the eighth grade, and the eleventh grade and asking the same questions; the only difference was the quality level. So we tried to break that, and that was very difficult to do. Some people quit teaching social studies. They were not comfortable with change; others thought it was wonderful. And we attracted a lot of teachers who were interested in that kind of thing. But, one key to that was continued in-service. And, when there were projects nationwide, we would get involved in them. For instance, there were projects at Stanford University for about four or five summers, and we always had a team of teachers there.

Because bringing about curricular reform was central to Cleo's understanding of herself as a teacher, I pushed to understand what role she saw herself playing in bringing about curriculum change.[8] Again, Cleo deferred her own agency as a curricular innovator. Simultaneously, despite this deferral, Cleo was involved in a massive restructuring of the curriculum; a huge project entailing many levels of organization and management. Her deferral seemed to signal another site in which she was negotiating her gendered subjectivity. If Cleo sees herself as enacting change, even while recognizing that this is not a proper role for women, then Cleo once again needs to do some fancy footwork. The conflicts Cleo might have experienced are revealed in the following quote by a fellow administrator, who perceived that he had 'inherited' Cleo as a result of district reshuffling. He described her job as,

> to see that resources were divided and curriculum administered . . . Cleo's job was to provide training and she was very, very good. She knew the resources, people, local as well as national. Our district became part of the National Consortium of Social Studies, and she provided some really valuable experiences for teachers and administrators.

Compared to other administrators, he commented that, 'Cleo was head and shoulders above other people. She could have been a principal or superintendent, but she was not into politics; you have to be an animal . . . Working with teachers and instruction; that was her thing.'

His comments reveal several layers of gendering. Administrators are political, they are animals, in other words male. Cleo on the other hand, worked with teachers (female). Although he suggests that Cleo was 'head and shoulders above others' and could have been a principal, he claims that she wasn't into that sort of thing. Thus he relegates her decision to not become a principal to her supposed disposition and not any discriminatory practices. His gendered perception that working with teachers is not a political act highlights the predominant view that change originates in the district office, not in the classroom. Working with teachers was central to Cleo's philosophy of bringing about change. I perceived this as an extremely political act, because I saw it as a form of subversion in which Cleo used the system ultimately to change the system.

Of course, when I asked Cleo to describe her role as a change agent she consistently replied by saying that I should get that information from those with whom she worked. The project was organized to try to incorporate the voices of all those impacted by the change. A representative committee of social studies educators from the district was formed. Margaret, an elementary social studies teacher, who served as the elementary representative to the curriculum committee for three years reflected,

> I remember Cleo was very good; she did things in a quiet way. In her quiet little way she went around to everyone, personalized the experience, came and talked to me, gave everyone a lot of leeway to express

themselves. I didn't have to 'toe the line' or didn't feel that anything was being imposed on me.

The area superintendent also commented that Cleo was best at 'helping people help themselves'.

As part of her work in chairing the curriculum committee, Cleo organized extensive in-service courses for teachers, summer workshop sessions, exchanges and programmes with other universities, including the local university, as well as the Ohio State University and Stanford University. These outreach programmes were primarily motivated by a desire to get more teachers involved in the process. Margaret believed strongly that part of Cleo's success was due to her ability to incorporate more and more people into the change process.

> Cleo believed you have to involve people. She got more and more people involved, the more you involve people who will be expected to change, the greater the chance of success. She realized that setting up curriculum from the top down just does not work. She organized all these workshops and got all these experts in the various social science disciplines together. She always had a motivational speaker to get us excited. I applied for a teacher exchange to England after one of these workshops because I was so excited. When the committee interviewed me for the Fulbright, their eyes lit up when I told them about the social studies project we were working on.

Cleo visited teachers in their classrooms, as well as continuing to teach one course herself in order to retain legitimacy among the teachers. She strongly believed that, 'If you don't keep your curriculum in touch with the classroom, it's not worth doing anything'.

Throughout her narrative Cleo decentralizes her role as a change agent. Rather than interpret this as the deference expected of women, I believe that embedded in Cleo's narrative is a different understanding of change, in which power must be decentralized in order for the collective investment necessary for change to occur. Central to her story of curricular change was the continual theme of getting teachers involved in in-service courses, summer workshops and exchange programmes with other universities, and incorporating the voices of teachers. For Cleo, change is not predicated on consolidation of power; rather change requires power to be dispersed through connections to others. As Lyn Nelson (1993) suggests, communities are primary epistemic agents, not the isolated subject positioned by traditional epistemology. For Cleo, change necessitates the creation of a context in which all those involved take responsibility for designing and implementing changes in curriculum. Thus, authority functions as a catalyst for attaining community and consensus rather than as a means for achieving and consolidating control. Cleo's leadership is not about controlling colleagues or imposing curriculum reforms; rather her goal is to facilitate.

However, when women administrators take on this role of being a facilitator, a term that is associated with women, there is a complex gender dynamic (Bloom and Munro 1995). As a facilitator, Cleo risks erasing herself as an expert, which in turn reproduces cultural norms that women are not creators of knowledge and should not have authoritative voices. Remember her supervisor's comment that 'she was not into politics . . . working with teachers that was her thing'. Cleo's work with teachers (facilitation) is not seen as political, whereas Cleo's own understandings of her actions imply that her work with teachers was political because it changed the very landscape (notions of power and authority) in which she and her colleagues functioned.

I do not mean to give 'epistemic privilege' to 'women's ways of knowing', which would only replicate the essentialist tendency I criticize. However, this story suggests that women do act in the world in ways that attempt to rewrite the plot written for women. For women, who often define themselves in terms of their connections with others (Belenky *et al.* 1986), the dispersal of power is central to establishing communities that are pivotal in developing collective investment in social change. This relational understanding of change, in which power is decentralized and dispersed, posits alternative epistemological frameworks from which women teachers constitute acts of agency. How women experience the process of change is central to understanding the conditions and culture of their work, as well as reconsidering traditional concepts of agency, change, power and resistance to suggest alternative ways of 'being' in the world not based on identity as unitary and male.

Reflections

For Cleo, retirement changed the content of her life, but not the pace. 'I'm not a person who wants quiet all the time. I taught school too long for that.' Her days are full, beginning with an early morning walk along the river and ending in the evening with work on her latest needlepoint project. Travel with friends and her monthly dinner gatherings with her group of former women colleagues are central components of her life.

The apparent simplicity of her life today seems to mask the complexity of her former professional life. Left out of this story almost completely is the other half of Cleo's life; her husband and son and her struggles to maintain a family life as well as a professional one. Cleo often stated that personal life and professional life should not be mixed. One thing you did not do was talk about family life at work. From her perspective it just was not professional. In any case, most of our discussions about her son and family took place after the tape recorder went off. I respect her decision not to talk about family during the formal part of our interview and her requests not to include certain stories. Like all stories, then, this one is partial.

As I began this study, an intended focus was change. How do women teachers bring about change in a hierarchical, patriarchal system in which they hold subordinate positions, which require or at least expect that they maintain the status quo? I was interested in how women teachers perceived the change process, if they perceived themselves as agents of change, how they sought to bring about change and the forms of resistance they encountered. This focus on women teachers as 'activists' stemmed from my desire to dispel the myth of teachers as passive, docile and submissive and portray them as active agents struggling against hegemonic constraints. I hoped to find, hidden under the cloak of respectability, political subversives working to transform the world.

Instead, I found women, like Cleo, who were quite willing to work within the educational system. They were trying to enact change through what I initially perceived to be conventional channels, rather than overthrow the system. Cleo's adamant belief that, 'I resisted, I didn't try to change things', was perplexing; it did not speak to my experience of myself as actively working towards change. Just as unsettling was my sense that Cleo and I did share a similar vision of what education should be and a strong belief in the purpose and need for change in social studies. Our different ways of naming our experiences highlighted our differences and made me keenly aware of the various ways in which we create realities.

In listening to Cleo's narrative, I found embedded in her story the struggle to name her own reality, to acknowledge the meanings she gives to her experiences in spite of the predominant assumptions regarding the nature and roles of women. Her narratives help us better to understand the meanings that teachers give to their work, and thus enlarge our understandings of teacher culture, but also ask us to suspend taken-for-granted notions of agency, resistance, knowledge and power; concepts central to the writing of the self. In doing so, we gain a glimpse of the complex ways in which meaning is made and the profound power relationships against which we write our lives. For Cleo, who could have 'lived another life and been just as happy', her narrative reminds me that my work is not about seeking any final interpretation but acknowledges that we are continually rewriting our pasts as a way to make sense of the present.

Notes

1 As Bloom (1996), S. Smith (1987) and Jacobs *et al.* (1995) suggest, narrative genres that reify a unitary hero-subject have the potential to impose a male master narrative on women, which ultimately works to erase gendered subjectivity.

2 Steedman (1990:245) maintains that the power of life histories is that they 'illuminate ideas, ideologies, class and gender relations, and social practices'.

3 At the same time that I read Cleo's narrative to understand how she constructs gender, I have simultaneously had to struggle to resist constructing a unitary tale. On one level, I romanticized Cleo's struggle to be independent and free of social norms and expectations. It was seductive to construct a female heroine. Yet, this unitary reading of Cleo as rebel, threatened to not only reproduce a male master narrative but to produce a singular, stable, unitary self. The inclination of both the narrator, as well as the researcher, to construct a coherent self is a strong one, which imposes an order on 'what is multiple and even disorderly' (Stewart 1994:30). Yet, the need to 'tell a good story and to summarize and define a person pushes us to represent them as unified persons'. As the Personal Narratives Group (1989:13) maintains, 'deeply embedded notions and expectations about the "normal" course of a life, as well as unconscious rules about what constitutes a good story, shape a personal narrative as much as the "brute facts" of existence do'.

4 On one level, this interpretation of Cleo's story situated Cleo as an active agent in that she knew how to manipulate playfully her gendered identity. And yet, the notion of masquerade, while suggesting the performative aspects of gender, and thus disrupting the essentializing aspects, was unsatisfactory to me. A mask suggests that something is being concealed. What is underneath the mask, what is being protected or concealed is suggestive of a 'true identity' (see Kaplan (1993) for a thought provoking discussion of masquerade). Thus, despite the allure of envisioning Cleo's grandmother as engaging in 'masquerade' I was suspicious of the ways in which notions of unitary subjectivity were still deeply embedded in notions of gender resistance as performing femininity. Cleo's narratives, in fact, did not allow for any tidy reading of gender.

5 I recognize now that my investment in Cleo's story was a means by which I could rewrite my own story, in which I had dealt with the realization of female devaluation by becoming more male. The recognition of this erasure, the negating of my identity, has made me profoundly aware of the misogyny of Western culture. To seek out narratives or stories of women who can negotiate patriarchy without the violence of erasure has been compelling for me.

6 Walkerdine (1990) reminds us that the discourse of teaching as 'women's true profession' situates women in an impossible fiction in which women's proclivity towards nurturing simultaneously valorizes and sabotages teachers' work.

7 This was during a period of social studies reform known as the new social studies.

8 Not only was Cleo connecting with curriculum reform projects at Stanford as well as Ohio State University, but she was also pursuing her own education at Teachers College Columbia, where she received her Masters degree.

4 Bonnie:
'Being a teacher is like being a fish out of water'

We sat comfortably in the kitchen of Bonnie's suburban home on a rainy Saturday morning during the dark winter months so characteristic of the Pacific Northwest. Black tea with plenty of freshly-squeezed lime, a Middle Eastern custom Bonnie learned from some of her Iranian students, helped to take off the chill. Bonnie reflected on lessons learned in her early twenties.

> I tend to be more people oriented. I understand what's going on between people a lot better now. I think I was naturally immuned to the landscape. And so, as it will turn out later, by beginning to look at the landscape and seeing and analyzing what's there, I began to see how certain things on the landscape are highly symbolic of lots of other things happening. I now understand that all of our cultural values are reflected somehow in landscapes.
>
> Landscapes can be read like a book, history is there, trade relations are there. Our space is important, what space is important, who gets it, what it's used for – all of these things make me much more observant about what's going on. Now when I travel, I not only look at the landscape, but I analyse it. In the end, I finally figured out, if you really want to know what people's cultural values are, you look at how they spend their time, what they do with their space, and what their money is spent on – time, space and money, rather than listening to what they say their happiness is.

Bonnie led me through her life, giving me markers such as 'it will turn out later' and 'in the end', which were supposed to signal the twists and turns in her life. She is a storyteller. Her tale of learning to 'read the landscape' is key to understanding Bonnie's life. Fitting for a geographer, she provided the map, although I was left to discover the path. Like a good teacher, Bonnie foreshadowed what was to come; I am left curious, wanting to hear more.

In contrast to Cleo, who 'didn't analyse her life', but 'just did it', I am intrigued with the degree of self-analysis Bonnie incorporates into her story.

Her suggestion that reality is deceptive and thus requires that one read and analyse the landscape are hard lessons learned. Keeping women 'immune' from reality is the traditional way in which women are protected and sheltered. The real world is hidden; mysterious; beyond our comprehension. We are not to 'read' the landscape, but are merely to be objects in it. Bonnie's story represents one woman's struggle to forge a path that acknowledges women as subjects, not objects, in the landscape of life. As a teacher, she hopes to teach students to read the landscape so they will actively engage in and understand the world around them.

Finding a fit

Born in 1945 and raised in Alberta, Canada, Bonnie, at 46 years old, considers herself part of the postwar baby boom. She describes her parents as typical of the World War II era. Retired for several years now, her parents spend much of their time travelling between home and their four children. During our first interview, she characterized her parents as 'gypsies' because of their tendency to pack up their things and move from day to day.

Despite her parents' current restlessness, Bonnie was raised and lived in the same small town throughout her childhood in Canada. School seems to have been a central and enjoyable experience for her. She recalled,

> I had some very, very interesting teachers. I ended up doing well in language and in social studies. Math and science were not areas I was really interested in. I was interested in some sciences, but mostly I enjoyed the history classes. I remember a writing assignment one teacher in the eleventh [grade] gave us. It was about democracy and I had written something about democracy not being able to operate very well unless the population was educated. And I remember him giving my paper back to me, and he said, 'You know, someone else had this same idea about 500BC'. And I said, 'No!' He said it was Plato.
>
> You know, that's a real striking thing he did; he reinforced what I had written – that there's wisdom in the past, that people have been writing about these kinds of subjects for a long time. I developed a real strong interest in the ideas that people were working with in the past, not just the course of history, but I was interested in what people were thinking about and what kinds of conclusions, what kind of knowledge base they had, and how those ideas changed over time. I have a strong interest in intellectual history. I'll sit down and read something like Thomas Paine; I am very curious about his ideas about Christianity. These are things that are interesting. I never have been able to read novels much.

At a young age Bonnie received validation for her intellectual abilities. Her interest in making connections between past and present, in understanding the evolution of philosophies, and in reading the works of intellectuals was nurtured and encouraged by her teachers. Bonnie attributes much of her interest in more 'intellectual' pursuits specifically to the encouragement of several male administrators,

> It seems to me that somewhere along the line I ended up involved in activities where administrators gave me a lot of positive reinforcement for my interests. In Canadian education, there was a fair distance between administrators and students . . . when I was in high school, the administrators were required to teach, so the principal and the vice principal ended up having a personal interest . . . I think they played a real important role in getting some of us who were females thinking and motivated to get more involved in English and social studies.

Gaining self-confidence in her academic abilities, particularly in social studies, a typically male discipline, and being acknowledged for her intellectual abilities seem to be central to Bonnie's emerging identity as a teenager. Like other adolescent girls, this period is usually characterized as one of differentiation: a search for one's own voice, establishing one's independence, and making one's own choices (Gilligan *et al.* 1990:260). Young girls raised to be caretakers and nurturers of relationships often find this a difficult time in which there is tension between their desire to maintain connections while also wanting to be independent. This period of differentiation is often fraught with conflicting messages regarding gender norms. On the one hand young women are to be 'feminine', and on the other, they are to be adolescents, a discourse defined primarily by male norms (Hudson 1984). These conflicting expectations were particularly salient for Bonnie and provide a site in which she negotiated her gendered subjectivity. This negotiation entailed taking up a subject position in which women could be thinkers and authorities, a subject position usually reserved for men, without relinquishing her own sense of self. It is through the story of her relationship with her father that this struggle was most clear.

> My father was one of those strong males who assumed that you can do whatever you want to do. He assumed that I was capable, that I would set high goals, and he had very high expectations of me. He expected me to measure up to those expectations, but I never quite measured up, which may be part of the self-doubt I also experience. It doesn't matter how good you are, there's still room to go further . . . I don't think you could ever accuse me of being over confident. I have never been over confident, whether it was in association work or whatever. To me, there can always be a surprise. I look at my track record, and I say, okay, whatever I really wanted to do, I was able to do. So I have that. But that's kind of intellectual. Emotionally, I think I am still fairly humble. I have doubts.

Despite Bonnie's own understanding of herself as smart and curious, she receives the message that she can 'never quite measure up'. Bonnie must negotiate the tension between her own self-image and cultural expectations of gender, in which never 'measuring up' can be interpreted as meaning that she has internalized the message that women will never be as good as men. Her uncertainty as to whether she could ever reach the elusive standard her father set created a self doubt, which reinforced cultural norms that sanction that women not have authoritative voices. The implicit message is that for women to be female is not to have authority. I believe Bonnie 'resisted' this by attributing her intellectual and analytical abilities to something intuitive, something outside her father's and other males' ability to criticize.

> I think I have good skills. How do I know where I got this ability to sense where things were politically? What to do to avoid problems, what to do to amend problems? I just don't know . . . so the only thing that I can think is that, to some degree, it comes from my education in history and political science. But there's something more than just knowing it . . . There's something about being able to feel it. I personally think it was my relationship with my father, because he was a power figure.

'It' seems to refer to understanding power and authority, which is the natural domain of men. 'My father was extremely authoritarian, and so I think I understood when people get their backs up. I had to learn ways to facilitate, in some instances, and in other instances, I went to the wall. So I had to find ways to get along most of the time with authority and be able to persevere.' Learning to 'get along' with authority (read father or patriarchy) not only signals Bonnie's understanding of dominant gender norms, but suggests that she actively pursued ways in which to negotiate these power relations in ways that would not erase her own sense of self. Part of learning to negotiate social relations seems to be the ability to distinguish the difference between authority or voice, and authoritarianism. This distinction is described in her early struggle to assert her voice:

> I guess I believe in strong authority, provided that it is authority that's used judiciously and that I can understand it and work with it. I can't understand authority for authority's sake, and I will challenge it. I think it goes back to the way in which I behaved with my father. When I thought he was wrong, I had the will. You can't imagine how much willpower I had. I believed that I was right and that he was wrong, and it didn't matter if he was an authoritarian figure or not . . .
>
> I can give you one example, when I was in college in 1968 during the civil rights movement. Racial issues were being debated on campus, and I thought, 'My parents brought me up not to discriminate, to not even point at someone to make them feel bad about something'. We just

learned those little things – don't point at somebody, don't eat candy in front of somebody unless you plan on sharing it . . . Then I got here in the United States – we'd been here a while. I had a boyfriend who was black, although I was never seriously interested in him; certainly he and I had spent some time together . . . My father said, 'You will not have that young man come to this house'. Well, if he didn't come to this house, that meant I had to meet him elsewhere.

His intent was for me to sever the relationship. I said, 'No, that isn't right'. He said, 'Well, you may not live here under those circumstances, because I will decide what happens under this roof'. And I said, 'Okay, so be it'. And I moved out. And that relationship was really fractured for about six months or so. Ultimately, he relinquished control of the situation. We never talked about the situation again . . . I never brought the subject up again. And, we have never talked about my absolute stand, because I thought he was wrong . . . I couldn't understand my parents. So I was real disappointed, but on the other hand, I thought they were wrong in principle. My mother did try and stay out of it. She would never have made it an issue like that. He made it an issue. So I was prepared not to ever see him again. Not to ever talk with him again. Fortunately, he backed off on that somewhat. He didn't think the issue was worth severing relationships with me forever.

Bonnie not only realizes that her sense of ethics are different from her father's, but experiences deep disappointment with the disjuncture between what she understood to be her father's values and his actions. She resists accepting authority for authority's sake by maintaining her confidence in her ability to determine right and wrong and act accordingly. In her words,

You see the thing about it is that I'm adamant. I'm tenacious. [When] I think they're extremely important issues . . . then I guess I'm willing to sacrifice a lot of things over these issues. My sister tells me to just, back off; you're not going to change anybody's mind by getting so adamant. In fact, she called me this morning and said, 'You know, you have a ten-dency when you think that you're right on the war [with Iraq] to alien-ate people when you get emotional about some of these things . . . To address the war with my father – he's a World War II person – you're not going to get anywhere. So why make it . . .?'. And of course, I can't help it, because, see, I grew up with the freedom to challenge, to go at it, to have it out. And these issues are important. We always argued about issues.

The arguments didn't really come to severing relationships . . . ; that's typical in my father's family. The females who married into the family used to hate family gatherings because it's all we did, and when I got old enough, I did it also, based on what I saw of my grandfather and his sons, who would be my father's brothers; they just loved to debate and argue, and they got heated. It was over anything from religion, politics, whatever.

In claiming her voice by participating in the debates usually reserved for men, Bonnie asserted her right to be heard, not silenced, in political and intellectual matters. To take up a position of authority while being judicious and not authoritarian (male) is the gender conflict Bonnie confronts.

As Bonnie told this story I connected immediately with what she was saying. I thought of my younger sister who stormed away from the dinner table when the conversation over topics like apartheid or nuclear weapons got heated. Although I always felt unsure, because I sensed I was not really being taken seriously, I wanted my voice to be heard in what I judged to be the really important discussions. In being included in the real conversations, I hoped to avoid the sense of alienation I often felt at being left out and excluded.

I wondered whether Bonnie's engagement in family debates was a similar experience of claiming her intellectual voice. For Bonnie, these forums provided a space to test her authority. 'My confidence comes from confrontation', she reflected. Bonnie's feeling was that, 'arguing doesn't sever relationships, ultimatums do'. Carol Gilligan and her colleagues (1990:20) suggest that, for women, disagreement can be a sign of relationship, a manifestation of two people coming together. It is in close relationships that girls are most willing to argue or disagree, trusting that those closest to them will listen and that they will try to understand.

In seeking to establish connection through confrontation, women who assert a public–intellectual voice subvert the gender norms, which suggest that women should subsume their own thoughts and feelings in order to nurture those of others. Not only have women in this society been denied an authoritative voice by virtue of being relegated to the private sphere, but women seeking to take part in public dialogue are seen as unnatural and problematic. Men who speak strongly about their beliefs are seen as assertive; women who speak strongly, as Bonnie's sister suggests, are seen as aggressive or emotional.

These early school and family experiences were central in shaping Bonnie's image of herself as an intellectual and facilitator. Her belief in herself and her ability to be judicious are closely linked to her strong beliefs regarding what is right and what is wrong. Bonnie continues to claim her voice today by engaging in 'debates' with her principal and the male faculty. My second visit at Bonnie's school coincided with the news that the USA had gone to war with Iraq. When I visited Bonnie over the following weeks we spent her planning periods in the faculty lounge with the principal and other male faculty debating US actions and motives in the Middle East. Bonnie strongly defended her view that the war was wrong and misguided by uninformed assumptions. I often wondered how she made the shift from these heated third-period debates in the faculty lounge to her world civilization class, in which her voice became one of questioner and facilitator. The classroom was one in which student voices were to be heard and challenged. Bonnie's commitment to student voices resulted in part from her own experiences in which her voice had been silenced. Maintaining her sense of authority and powerfulness was an ongoing theme in her emergent understanding of herself as an 'activist', to which I now turn.

The 'do-gooder'

The sixties was fertile ground for social change. I didn't understand the civil rights issues at all because I was never exposed to anything like that in Canada. I didn't understand black culture. I didn't understand that there were slums. What was happening in the United States was completely divorced from anything that I knew. I mean I could only understand it intellectually. And, for me, I like to have more than that. I like to be able to try and understand it by some kind of experience with it. And that might also have something to do with the way I teach.

Like Cleo's adolescent recollection of Atlanta's 'mill town' and her realization that 'I didn't know there were people like that', Bonnie also expresses her awakening to social injustices. Bonnie's young adulthood, during college and early teaching years, were a time in which her own sense of authority and voice were challenged. Two primary events, joining VISTA and participating in a strike, provided the actual experiences that not only reinforced her convictions of social responsibility, but cultivated her skills in political action.

After Bonnie's first year in college at the University of Alberta, Edmonton, she decided, 'If I don't move now and see the world, I am probably never going to see the world'. It was 1965; Bonnie's father had moved to the Pacific Northwest and suggested that Bonnie come and attend the University of Oregon. She recalled that, with so much happening in the USA, it seemed like a very exciting thing to do.

I went to see Hurbert Humphrey at the University of Oregon campus. He gave a talk about the war on poverty . . . that we are required to take some responsibility . . . Some groups were anti-war. There was another group that was more interested in dropping out of society, the flower children. The one that I tied into required a social imperative, like in Michael Harrington's book, about the 'other America', the invisible America, where you don't come in contact with the poverty that exists in America . . . Those all made a[n] impression on me, and after hearing Hubert Humphrey and reading Michael Harrington and others, I decided to join VISTA and specify that I wanted to work in the urban south, in the black ghetto somewhere, and try to understand what was going on there, to know what all this terror is about. So then you can imagine: I ended up in Atlanta, Georgia, at the time Martin Luther King Jr was organizing, where Stokely Carmichael had just incited a riot, and a large portion of Atlanta burned down.

Bonnie had the choice to go to school in England for a year on a school exchange or join VISTA. In the end she decided, 'I could always go to school in England, but I can't always have this kind of experience in the south'. She recollected her motivations and those of her peers.

I think in some ways you could probably say we were all 'do-gooders'. You know, there to do something, anything . . . But I was there to learn as much as to do something socially, but I was very, very interested in trying to understand what was going on and why it was going on. I think I was a bit idealistic, too. Can we change the world?

After what she called her 'indoctrination' into the VISTA program, Bonnie was assigned to a project called 'Perry Homes' in the heart of Atlanta and in the heart of poverty. She described her work with VISTA.

I was assigned to an all black housing project and my job was to work with Planned Parenthood. One of the obvious problems was that frequently you'd go into a household and there would be three women of child-bearing age, all with children, and an absence of males in these homes, which were extremely poor and yet had fairly large numbers of children.

What we were trying to do was knock on doors to see if we could get these people to trust us, to be invited in, to get them to understand, that, first of all, we were there to collect information about how many people were in the household, and who was related to whom. And also to get them to understand what kind of services were available, not only in Planned Parenthood, but in nutrition services and children's services, which were being offered by the government at that time. We wanted them to get to know what services were available and how to get assistance. With regards to Planned Parenthood, they wanted us to get them to work with a nurse and become educated about birth control.

Bonnie recounted what a powerful experience it was to be accepted into the homes of these black women. 'What I remember is being received, and the friendliness . . . Whether or not these people later came in, utilized the services, and saw the nurse, I have no idea.' Her success was not measured by how many women she persuaded to go to Planned Parenthood, but on connections she formed and the relationships she developed. These were essential to gaining a real understanding of the issues of the day.

Despite her success, at the end of the training period in Atlanta, Bonnie was told by 'VISTA officials who had come down from Washington' that she must return to Oregon. The reason they gave for her early dismissal was that she was being 'unwittingly seductive'. Bonnie explained,

> They said that they were concerned for my safety as a white woman . . . I had long hair and I suppose in the sixties I wore clothes that were short; they seemed quite normal to me . . . A number of their psychologists were very concerned about white, fairly attractive women being in black areas and . . . being at risk. So they called me in one day and just as quickly as you could snap your finger, they said, 'You're going back to Oregon today'.

Under the pretext of concern for her, the 'officials' (male bureaucrats) impose the right of patriarchy which situates women as in need of being protected. On another level, Bonnie learns implicitly that women are not to be in the public sphere, to be activists. Women in the public sphere disrupt the natural order.

The fact that she had never encountered any problems with black men and did not feel in danger, made it difficult for Bonnie to understand the decision of VISTA to send her back to Oregon.

> To me, it was sort of like hitting your head against a brick wall asking what is it that you're talking about? . . . Because I do have to say that a lot of the women who joined VISTA, I think they were diverted by other things that had to do with their social life . . . and these other girls would kind of run around with these guys. And I didn't do any of that stuff and I thought what are you guys talking about here . . . It's like, I couldn't understand what it was that they were getting at.

Bonnie's clear sense of social responsibility and her understanding of her motivations are in conflict with others' interpretations of her actions as being 'unwittingly seductive'. Her authority to name her experiences is discounted. As a result of this juxtaposition, Bonnie seems to suffer from what Sandra Bartky (1990:18) refers to as 'double ontological shock'; the realization that what is really happening is quite different from what appears to be happening, and the frequent inability to comprehend what is really happening at all. This self-doubt can heighten one's awareness to the full extent of sex discrimination in its most subtle forms, coinciding with what Bartky (1990:18) calls 'wariness', resulting in compliance with socially sanctioned norms of behaviour through a process of self-regulation in an attempt to avoid the male gaze. In this mode women are in a constant state of anticipation and apprehension at the possibility of attack. This experience, in which Bonnie believes herself to have been treated unfairly, reinforced her belief in the need to take an active role, especially for the rights of women.

After her dismissal from VISTA Bonnie returned to Oregon to complete her secondary degree in education at the University of Oregon. To help pay for tuition fees, Bonnie waitressed in 'a really fancy restaurant' in town. During this time, the restaurant workers went on strike and Bonnie was asked to join the union. She explained that she didn't understand the need for a strike. 'It was really low wages, but I got really good tips there. Some of the tips those gentlemen gave me, I was a little concerned with, but, as it turned out, it was never a problem. They wanted to help this young lady going back to college in Oregon.' She recalled that her boss encouraged her not to join the union and even suggested how she might go about getting rid of the union altogether. When her fellow workers informed her that it was illegal for the boss to discourage her from joining the union, she began to see the broader picture.

> I learned from the strike. I formed friendships with people who were working for very little. Lots of them were old time employees. They were older women who had worked there for a long time, and they were people who were struggling. What I used my tips for was to go to school, pay tuition, buy books. They used their tips to pay for medical plans and for child care . . . These people tried to explain to me, naive as I was, why they needed to have this union . . . I began to suspect that I lived in a world other than the world of those of us being educated . . . So I thought, it [the union] makes sense to me. These women need this medical plan. And it seems to me that the owners should be able to pay for it. So, I became an activist.

Bonnie joined the union, went on strike, walked the picket line and in fact stuck it out the longest. While the other waitresses eventually had to find other work, Bonnie and her boyfriend remained on strike until they were the last ones picketing outside the restaurant, encouraging patrons to boycott it. Management never gave in, and Bonnie went down the street to work for another restaurant. Although they did not win the strike, Bonnie's comment at the end of it all was, 'One of the things that I learned from was the friendships I formed with people . . . I was fortunately gaining experience with people who really had to struggle and work for a living.'

Her experiences going on strike and with VISTA were central to Bonnie's emerging identity as an activist and especially as an advocate of women. In both cases, Bonnie's work on behalf of, and with, other women, met with opposition. Women are often expected to take up this work of being the 'do-gooder' and yet when this role extends into the public sphere women are once again reminded that they should not have authoritative, public voices. For Bonnie the negotiation of her own self-understanding as judicious and being an activist conflicts with gender norms. This negotiation of conflicting subjectivities would later be taken up again when she joined the Teachers' Association. Her role as activist and advocate were central to Bonnie's understanding of what it means to be a teacher. These understandings are in direct opposition to dominant cultural expectations of teachers. This site of gender conflict resulted in Bonnie saying repeatedly that being a teacher was like being 'a fish out of water'.

Learning to teach: 'finding a fit'

Because Bonnie framed her story of entering teaching within the context of her work as a union organizer and as a VISTA volunteer in the south during the civil rights movement, I initially interpreted her decision to be a teacher as another form of social activism. Captured by the agency of her story, which I initially interpreted as subverting the patriarchal narrative for women, I was surprised by Bonnie's description of her path into teaching. She recalled her decision to enter teaching in the early 1970s. 'There weren't many alternatives and it was the beginning of the baby boom and lots of us were graduating in teaching.' Like Cleo, she defers her decision to others, and invokes the dominant ideology that teaching is women's true profession by suggesting that 'there weren't many alternatives'. I wondered what role telling this fiction played. Why would Bonnie tell the story that 'there weren't many alternatives', when in fact, clerical, nursing and other professions were open to women. As Jo Anne Pagano (1990:195) suggests, creating a fictionalized self is not a lie or masquerade but, in itself, a theoretical construct. Stories or fictions become a form of agency through which women can 'dispense with boundaries' (Jagla 1992:62) that circumscribe their lives. Thus, in the case of Bonnie, the fiction that there weren't many alternatives allowed her to take up an identity as a teacher. Bonnie's story of teaching revealed to me how engaging hegemonic ideologies functioned as a form of resistance, despite my understanding of resistance as a word that implied opposition. I imagined that engaging the ideology of teaching as 'women's true profession' allowed Bonnie to reconcile conflicting images of herself as activist with dominant images of teachers as passively enacting women's natural nurturing capacity. The telling of this fiction allows Bonnie to redefine teaching without doing so in ways that perpetuate dominant gender norms.

Despite her negotiation of the gender conflicts represented in her decision to become a teacher, Bonnie's initial ambivalence towards teaching is reflected in her continual negotiation between her own self-image as political activist (male) and do-gooder (female), and the roles prescribed by patriarchy, which suggest that women should not have an authoritative, public voice. Her understanding of herself as a political activist was reflected in her commitment to protecting teachers' rights and acknowledging teachers' agency through association work. She recalled:

> The Teachers' Association was important to me. It was my high priority. Kids and marriage were my low priority. Men want women to fit

into their lives. I was trying to create something separate and distinct, not fit into someone else's life. I chose not to have children. I could never envision myself with children. I always had all these other things to do.

For Bonnie, stepping outside, creating 'something separate' and not fitting into 'someone else's life' allowed her to move 'out of one's place' as bell hooks (1990:145) describes it, and into a space where she can 'confront the realities of choice and location'. By reinscribing teaching with her understanding of herself as activist she 'displaces' the patriarchal norms inscribed in teaching. Trinh Minh-ha (1991:21) suggests that 'displacing is a way of surviving', for in displacing ourselves, 'we never allow this classifying world to exert its classificatory power'. Like Cleo's use of the metaphor the 'drifter', as a means of displacing gender norms, Bonnie creates a space from which she can envisage herself as a teacher and an activist. In this way Bonnie negotiates the conflicted gender terrain of becoming a teacher.

And yet, despite the priority she gave to the Teachers' Association and her resistance to fitting into someone else's life, Bonnie confronted the tension between her own sense of agency and cultural expectations of appropriate gender behaviour. At the end of her first year of teaching, she moved to Portland to be with her boyfriend. While looking for a teaching job, she 'had to make a decision about whether or not to get married'. Despite her confidence in herself as a teacher, she reflected, 'I think I got married to be respectable as a teacher'. She described her wedding in Reno as,

a little two minute ceremony at the courthouse . . . I'm not very ritualistic. I never went to my own graduation in college . . . I didn't want any rituals associated with marriage . . . Mind you, this is in view of the fact that I'm observing Japanese rituals over the last three years. But I don't personally have a . . . I mean I thought they were just practices and they don't have much meaning for me personally. I just enjoy them as cultural attributes.

To be respectable is to conform to the marriage plot. Unmarried women teachers are suspect, they are not 'fitting' into gender norms, they are a threat. The tension that Bonnie feels in wanting not to 'fit in' and at the same time the expectations that women will comply with the marriage plot is evident in her ambivalence towards her own wedding. Her first and second marriages ended in divorce. She talked about her struggles to maintain both a full-time career and marriage, even without children. 'I have a wonderful relationship with men, as long as I don't get married to them. I just didn't run my life around my marriages. I always had my own life and I'm not sure men are ready to deal with the notoriety of their spouses.' For Bonnie, finding the fit between work and marriage that felt right was problematic. Bonnie clearly experiences the pressure of patriarchy to 'fit in' and conform to dominant gender norms, which maintain that women do not have authority. She counters this by her self-representation as an 'activist' and do-gooder, in which she appropriates the role of woman as care-taker, and simultaneously reinscribes it with her own understandings of what it means to be an activist. As a teacher she continually negotiates the dissonance between her own self-image as activist and do-gooder, someone who can actively bring about change, and the beliefs embedded in a patriarchal society.

Although teaching has been characterized as 'women's true profession', it does not follow that women have defined the field. In fact, on the contrary, teaching has functioned as a primary site through which to regulate normative gender expectations. Consistent with her experiences with VISTA and working in the union, as a teacher Bonnie experienced a severe disjuncture between her own self-understanding as an activist with a voice of authority and the sanctioning of that behaviour because it crossed the gender line. In the following section, I describe the regulation of the body as one way in which Bonnie's gender transgression was regulated.

Becoming an advocate for women teachers

In autumn 1990 Bonnie began her twenty-first year at Stevenson High School. A suburban high school lying in the hills outside a major city in the Pacific Northwest, Stevenson High School was selected as one of the nation's outstanding secondary schools in the US Department of Education's National Secondary Schools Recognition Awards program. Stevenson is one of two high schools serving a district with nine elementary schools, two junior high schools, and 375 teachers. It serves a middle- to upper-middle-class, white collar, professional community, which in the words of the superintendent, values 'success, results and work'.

Stevenson prides itself on providing a comprehensive academic programme. More than 80 per cent of the students at Stevenson High School go on to college. Seventy-eight per cent of the students take the Scholastic Achievement Test (SAT) exam, with scores averaging well above the national norm. The principal at Stevenson summarized it this way; 'the average kid has a difficult time here'.

Bonnie's life at Stevenson High School extends well beyond being a teacher. In addition to teaching a variety of courses in the social studies department, including global awareness, western civilization, US history and, more recently, the political action class, Bonnie was involved in, and was president of, the Teachers' Association, is an active member in the National Council for the Social Studies as well as the Geography Alliance, and is currently serving as department chair. She is described by colleagues as 'an excellent and innovative teacher'. The superintendent contended that there is 'no one I can think of who gets kids more involved'. In my mind there is no doubt that Bonnie represents the best of what education has to offer. These tidy descriptions, however, once again mask the complex and negotiated nature of Bonnie's work.

A primary site in which Bonnie grapples with conflicted subjectivities is in her understanding of herself as a teacher advocate. As Bonnie talked of her early teaching years, she focused on her work with the Teachers' Association. Bonnie has always been on the side of the teacher. She characterizes herself as a 'teacher–advocate'. Her strong belief in protecting teachers' rights and acknowledging teachers' professional judgement was a primary motivation in her early association work.[1] This was not always the case, as Bonnie recalls.

> When I first started teaching, I was very anti-association. I said 'What kind of deal is this?' Remember my strike experience? Well, what I learned in college was that the NEA [National Education Association] was the world's largest and the most ineffective organization, so I thought, well, why should I belong to this organization and all those teachers at Stevenson said I should. Even the principal told me that I should join the association . . . so for the first two years, the principal harangued me by telling me it was my professional duty to join this organization. I saw it as pro-administration, and it was; it was run by the administrators. I couldn't understand why should I pay these dues? I mean, what's the point here? Then these women who had been work-ing in the association for a long time, got a hold of me and they said, 'well, if you don't like the way things are, don't you think you should join and change things? Why don't you do something about this if you don't like the way things are.' Wrong thing to say to me.

With the encouragement of several women who were convinced that Bonnie would be 'really good', she went from being an 'ordinary teacher right from the building straight to the negotiating team'. She reflected on her success, which included averting a strike and successfully leading the association through a year-long negotiation process. 'I think I have some instincts that are political which I don't know where I got them but I understand power to some degree. I can feel it and understand it. Maybe it has to do with the power struggle I always had with my father, I'm not sure. But I understood it quite well.' Although Bonnie has not worked directly in the association for several years, she continues to believe in the need for a strong association, especially for women teachers;

> most teachers coming out of the university, even now, I think, they don't understand these relationships at all. I think women who are interested in teachers moving in this different direction of controlling their own contracts . . . [that is] establishing teacher rights, should not just be going over there and begging for whatever, and leaving control always in the hands of whether or not you have a good administrator.

Bonnie's commitment to teacher rights and autonomy is a form of resistance to gender norms. She resisted any administrators' attempts to control the aspects of classroom teaching that threatened to undermine the integrity of teachers. Two examples were in regard to grading and cheating. Bonnie did not feel administrators should have absolute veto power over a teacher's grade, nor in deciding whether a student had cheated. Bonnie believed that administrators, who weren't in touch daily with the classroom or students, were not qualified to make such decisions simply because they were the 'authority'.

Bonnie's early experiences with administrators, especially her first principal at Stevenson, seem to have heightened her awareness of unjust and sexist behaviour in schools, and the need for women not to leave things in the hands of administrators. She described her first principal;

> he preferred very strong willed, assertive women and usually reasonably attractive. His confident and patronizing way of dealing with people got him in all kinds of trouble and I guess I was one of those. I didn't take well to authority for authority's sake. It seemed to everyone, whoever he encountered, that he lacked certain skills. He seemed superficial . . . there is an example of this. One time he set up this chart with stars on it for what we thought were ridiculous things, like the number of times we did or didn't get to faculty meetings on time. I mean trivial things that just used to irk us terribly. One time, it was about the time that women had just gotten the right to wear slacks to school, and so dress codes were a big issue with him. Well, I always had problems with my feet swelling up because I always stand up when I teach, and it was hot so we'd wear sandals. Well, we'd wear open-toed sandals and he thought that was very unprofessional so he had Mickey [a fellow teacher] counsel with me; he had our administrator in charge of our department counsel with me; . . . he even called me in and he told me that I could wear these little toe things that Japanese wear with their thongs. These are the things that he spent a great deal of time and energy pursuing and it just used to irritate everybody.

Sandra Bartky points out (1990:26) that when body parts are separated out from the rest of a woman's personality and reduced to the status of mere instruments or else are regarded as if they are capable of representing women, this becomes sexual objectification. The control of women's bodies, which for women teachers has meant dress codes, becomes the apparatus through which women begin to turn the male gaze on themselves.[2]

As my colleague Leslie Bloom and I have discussed (Bloom and Munro 1995) common among women teachers' narratives were stories of the regulation of the body as a site of gender identity. As Foucault (1984) maintains, it is through the body that regulation and discipline occur. For women, the female body is both the subject and object for discipline by male bodies.

Bonnie's feet became the site for her principal's discomfort with the female body; a body that should be covered, so that the transgression of the female body into spaces usually reserved for and defined by men will be less apparent. The self-regulation women are expected to practice in regards to their bodies is apparent in a comment Bonnie's superintendent made.

> I expect to be challenged by her, she is a passionate person, committed to a deeply felt belief system . . . Bonnie would never use her sexuality to get what she wanted . . . twenty per cent of the female staff would use it, consciously or unconsciously, I might use my humour or boyish charm, but Bonnie would not approve of this.

To use her sexuality is in this case symbolic of her femaleness. Thus, according to the superintendent, Bonnie participates in the self-regulation of her sexuality. Leslie Bloom and I (1995:108) maintain that,

> as members of the workforce in a patriarchal society, women are expected to be productive within the construct of normative male productivity and professional behaviors; however to achieve this norm, they must be disciplined . . . This discipline serves to remind women that they may not speak or be present in public spheres as women.

When Bonnie asserts a public, authoritative voice, as she does through her advocacy of teachers' rights, the control and regulation of her body (as was also the case with her VISTA experience in which she was accused of being 'unwittingly seductive') is a reminder that women are bodies first, and people second.

The recent push for the professionalization of teaching, which has included the adoption of a business style of dress (i.e. 'dress for success' with high-collared blouses and bow-ties) becomes one more form of objectification and control through which normative femininity is inscribed. Women's bodies become a site through which gendered norms are maintained. The notion of professionalization functions as another form of control in which women must take on characteristics of men in order to be seen as professional. This form of self-erasure becomes a profound site of gender conflict and fragmented subjectivity. Avoiding self-erasure is nowhere more apparent than in Bonnie's role as an administrator.

A pain to administrators

To be a woman administrator is continually to negotiate gender roles. To be female is not to have authority. Thus, to be a female administrator is a contradiction in terms. To be recognized as a competent administrator, women must resist presenting themselves in stereotypically female ways. As women socialized to cultural femininity, becoming authoritative in ways that patriarchy socializes men is rife with conflicts; it may mean that they participate in their own exclusion and silence their own gendered voices (Pagano 1990). How Bonnie struggles to be seen as a competent administrator while not 'disappearing' is the focus of this section.

In autumn 1990, Bonnie became the department chair of an all-male social studies department. As both she and her principal remarked on separate occasions, 'blood was spilled' over that decision. Bonnie explained the controversy. 'There might have been some fear in an all-male department. I think they were not looking forward to me moving out of the teaching position I had been in for 15 years.' The department is characterized by others in the school as 'traditional', 'conservative' and 'old guard'. Bonnie's newest colleague in the department, a young woman whom Bonnie hired, commented 'you couldn't pay me to have Bonnie's job'.

In as much as her social studies colleagues may have attempted to block her promotion, Bonnie credits other males, particularly her principal, for helping her get it. 'Some men are willing to give assertive women the help they need and encouragement to move into leadership positions . . . Some of these men have put me out in front, and they've always been there to say, "we'll give you whatever support you need".' As department chair and part of the administrative team, Bonnie continually confronts stereotypical masculinist expectations of how to express power and authority: assumptions of hierarchy as natural, power as consolidation and authority as the willingness of others to give up their power. In contrast, Bonnie's understandings of power go back to her experiences with her father in which she, 'believed in strong authority, provided that it is authority that is used judiciously and I can understand it and work with it. I can't understand authority for authority's sake.' Authority should be achieved through judicious use of power, and therefore, misuse of authority should be confronted.

But, confrontation, as Bonnie defines it, is often misunderstood. For her, it is a means to talk through differing standpoints on issues with colleagues. That the talk may get confrontational does not trouble Bonnie, who assumes that, when colleagues differ, they do so based on commitments to principles and deeply held beliefs. Therefore Bonnie believes it is critical to talk through differences in order to understand another's standpoint. 'It takes a long time to develop the kind of trust that you can have different points of view, but that doesn't necessarily mean you're working with the enemy.'

As Carol Gilligan and her colleagues (Gilligan *et al*. 1990) suggest, for some women, disagreement or confrontation can be a sign of relationship because it indicates the desire to understand the position of the other. However, Gilligan's perspective conflicts with dominant ideology, in which women are expected to subsume their own thoughts in order to nurture those of others rather than to confront them for greater understanding. This became a concern in Bonnie's interview for department chair;

even in the interview, one of the things that they asked was 'what happened if your department wanted to go one way on an issue and the
administration would be opposed to it or have a different view, what
would you do?' I said, 'you mean, "no" isn't negotiable? I mean are you
assuming you don't have a good reason for the position that you're
taking?'

I sensed two different understandings of the purpose of dialogue. Bonnie
took seriously her commitments to personal values and if there were differences these could be talked through. Her understanding of confrontation is
a situation in which you trust someone enough to know you can disagree.
For many of her male colleagues their interpretation of Bonnie as confrontational suggests that she is engaging in a power struggle and is consequently
a threat.

Bonnie's work in the association has garnered her the reputation of being
a real 'teacher–advocate' and, from the perspective of the superintendent, as
'seeing change as confrontational'. His perception is that Bonnie does not
believe in collaboration, but sees confrontation as the only way to bring
about change. Bonnie agreed with his assessment of her as teacher–advocate, but does not see herself as confrontational in a negative way,

> I have to say that I had a reputation district wide, and other places too,
> and actually . . . wherever I had to go, to help teachers. I think those are
> very important steps to have established. But they think I was exceed-
> ingly confrontational. I did my homework and I was very good at it. It
> was real hard to maintain good relationships while you're in that kind
> of a role. I think they always did respect me and I have respect for those
> who I encounter, for the most part. But I think that that reputation
> keeps emerging.

Bonnie's active role in the political process in the district defies the gender
ideal of woman as nurturer, which Sandra Bartky (1990:100) suggests
requires that women find satisfaction in the satisfaction of others and that
they place their needs second in the case of conflict. Rather than placing her
needs and those of women teachers second, Bonnie asserts her strong convictions. Defying the expectation that she avert conflict, Bonnie becomes
suspect of not really understanding the political process. As the superintendent stated, 'what Bonnie is really good at is engagement; how well she
understands infrastructure is what I question'. He described Bonnie as a
'doer' not a 'reflector', she 'will focus on principles and not on the necessity
of getting broader community support'.[3]

When women do not repress disagreement or when they openly challenge
'misuse of authority' they are considered aggressive and unnatural. Consequently, Bonnie's often confrontational style and her challenges to authority
were interpreted in her school district as resistance to building consensus

rather than as efforts to forge relationships and gain deeper insights into differing standpoints.

Thus, as Bonnie negotiates her role as an administrator with what she believes is an appropriate manner to manifest authority in productive ways, she is cast into the devalued and disdained role of 'the aggressive female'. However, what Bonnie may be approaching in her desire for open, albeit confrontational dialogue is the basis for a notion in which power is not used to consolidate authority but to disperse authority in order to enlarge a group's collective investment in change.

Reflections

Although 'much blood was shed', after four months as chair Bonnie had successfully initiated some real change in the department, including: doing a participatory budget; conducting all-staff computer workshops; arranging for four teachers to go to the National Social Studies conference (the first time in 20 years that teachers have attended); and generally bringing the social studies department into the mainstream of school life. The principal is extremely pleased with Bonnie and says that the 'battle' was well worth it. 'Bonnie has an agenda and she systematically takes care of details to make things happen. She is a real team player and recognizes that she needs support . . . her bucket holds a lot of sand and we are using her talent as a leader.' In talking about her current relationship with the administration Bonnie reflected,

> They're sitting back and assessing my enthusiasm, my ability to work with kids . . . maybe I'm dependent upon other people to assess what skills I have and sort of draw me into certain situations. I sort of rely on other people to identify where my skills are and to say, here's an open door and would you like to pursue this, or we think you can do this.

Thus, despite her own strong sense of self, Bonnie experiences intense self-doubt. I conclude Bonnie's story on what I consider an ominous note. I sense that in her new position as department chair, Bonnie is at a juncture where she will recreate her role as activist and advocate. Her new role shaped the context for my view of Bonnie, my understanding of her at this particular point in time, and the focus of this story.

This story is thus, admittedly, partial. There are a great many omissions – the rare quality of her classroom teaching, her love of travel, and the women she considers to be her allies. What I have included are the stories that helped me to better understand my own experiences as a teacher. I resonated with Bonnie's self-image as an activist and intellectual. It spoke to my understanding of why I went into teaching. Her struggles to assert her authority as a teacher reminded me of what I perceived to be my double oppression as a woman teacher. I was not only a teacher, a professional of low status, but also a woman. Bonnie's story spoke to my understanding of how women teachers traverse from the world of the classroom, where we create the space to enact our own realities, to the world outside the classroom, in which we are too often left with no voice at all.

Notes

1 Teacher strikes 'plagued' state schools in the 1960s and 1970s. See Urban (1989) for an overview of teacher activism in this period.
2 Despite the attempts to regulate the female body, I would maintain that Bonnie's telling of these stories reflects her awareness of the forms of regulation that she has experienced. Consequently, this regulation is subverted. As Smith (1993a:131) suggests in regard to women's autobiographical practice, 'Writing her experiential history of the body, the autobiographical subject engages in a process of critical self-consciousness through which she comes to an awareness of the relationship of her specific body to the cultural "body" and to the body politic. That change in consciousness prompts cultural critique.'
3 The superintendent's understanding of Bonnie is ironic in light of the fact that Bonnie was the teacher of the 'hottest course' at Stevenson High School, which was the political action course, specifically aimed at getting students to understand the political process first hand.

5   Rewriting a life

The multiple and often contradictory subject positions taken up in these narratives preclude a single interpretation of the life histories of these three women teachers. As Joanne Pagano (1990) reminds us, 'there is more than one way to tell a story and more than one story'. A single interpretation of a life history is not only impossible, but undesirable, and to suggest that I can provide some final interpretation of these life history narratives would be an act of violence. Crapanzano (1980) reminds us that interpretation can be understood as a phallic, cruel, violent, and destructive act as well as a fertile, fertilizing, fruitful and creative one. How to reach some sort of conclusion without engaging in the violence of interpretation is the contradiction with which I engage. Rather than posit final truths, I hope to engage in a discussion that questions unitary readings of concepts like gender, resistance, subjectivity and agency.

As Madeline Grumet (1991) suggests, the ways in which we tell our stories are negotiations of power relations. How we speak our world is a political act. Agnes claims her lived experience as fluid rather than as static by maintaining that it is 'who you are, not what you teach'. Cleo, by suggesting that 'she could have lived another life and been just as happy', resists any coherent reading of her life. Bonnie's image of learning to read the landscape suggests her astute understanding of the interpretive and shifting nature of living a life. In constructing self-representations that decentralize a unitary self these women contest gender norms. Their narratives suggest the fictive nature of the woman subject. In continually disrupting notions of a unitary self the narratives suggest that meaning can be political only when it does not let itself be easily stabilized.

When I began this research I had hoped to identify modes of resistance that contested dominant images of women teachers as complicit in 'pedagogy for patriarchy' (Grumet 1988). What I had not anticipated was that my grounding in neo-Marxist and liberal feminist social theory was inadequate to explain these women's forms of agency. My assumptions regarding resistance were made apparent when the life historians' narratives did not 'fit' into my neat theoretical categories (Munro 1995b). By looking for 'acts' of resistance I reproduced notions of agency as public, power as possession and subjectivity as unitary (as either an oppressor or the oppressed).

In retrospect, my desire to collect the life histories of women teachers was certainly a response to my need to understand my own decision to go into teaching; a profession in which women are valorized for nurturing and, thus, simultaneously situated for oppression. I hoped, like others (Pinar 1983; Grumet 1988; J. Miller 1989), to rewrite the traditional script in which the female teacher submissively ushers girls and boys into the world of patriarchy. In collecting their life histories, I had initially wanted to 'give voice' to women teachers' stories of resistance. Taking for granted that women's resistance would be covert (and thus previously undiscovered and untheorized), lest they risk the very positions from which they could enact change, I sought to recover the stories of women teachers who identified themselves as political subversives. I felt confident that I would be able to rewrite the traditional gender plot. My focus on teachers as activists took up the claim made by others (Hoffman 1981; Kaufman 1984; Casey 1993) that teachers entered the profession for a variety of reasons, including bringing about social change.

Although a liberation narrative of social change disrupts the traditional tale of teachers' compliance with dominant gender expectations for entering teaching, this counternarrative also functions to reproduce a masculinist narrative of independence and autonomy. The characters change, but the plot lines remain deeply gendered as male. This focus on women teachers as subversives came from my desire to dispel the myth of teachers as passive, docile and submissive and portray them as active and committed agents struggling against hegemonic constraints. The image of the activist teacher popularized by heroes like Conrak, and terms like 'transformative intellectuals' (Giroux 1988) were seductive. The teacher was transformed from a passive woman to an active, revolutionary hero, who sought to 'save the children'. Save the children from who? In part, it was from women teachers.

In my desire to interpret teachers' stories as resistance, I now realize that I was in fact imposing another fiction. I had hoped to fit women into the current theoretical discourse and extend the neo-Marxist–postmodern discussion regarding the role of negotiation and resistance in understanding the relationship between individual actions and hegemonic constraints (Apple 1979; Giroux 1983; Wexler 1987). Initially, my reading of these women teachers' stories was grounded in a neo-Marxist understanding of resistance as public, active and oppositional. Grounded in Enlightenment notions of change, the individual and progress, resistance theory reproduces notions of the individual as autonomous, and change as linear and public. Yet, these teachers' stories did not conform to traditional notions of power as opposition, subjectivity as unitary, and resistance as public. Their stories did not 'fit' my initial goal of placing women's lives within 'resistance theories'. The absence of women teachers' voices from these discourses was not only an example of the continued marginalization of women, but also revealed how this very discourse functioned to exclude the experiences of women through its limited definitions.

Ironically, it was the life historians' resistance to the naming of themselves as subversives and often their denial of gender oppression, either as women or teachers, that prompted me to rethink the concept of resistance. I now understand their refusal to 'name' themselves subversives as a form of resistance through which they contested the dominant masculinist narrative, which defines power from a phallocentric world view, in which power is understood to be monolithic and a possession to be seized and acquired. As women in a patriarchal society, their refusal to acknowledge dominant power relationships signified their understanding of exclusion from these power relationships and represented an attempt to subvert their reproduction. In refusing to name themselves subversives, they deconstruct the dichotomies of active–passive and male–female, which reify dominant gender discourses. Naming, the usual right of the patriarch, proffers the right to determine identity and fate (Mackethan 1990). Refusal to 'take up identities' (Riley 1989), in this case as resistors, becomes an act of agency through which they become subjects. This refusal highlights forms of resistance usually obscured when resistance is understood to be reactive acts of opposition that operate outside the forces of power.

I now question whether the very naming of myself as an 'activist' is yet another example of the way in which patriarchy actually functions to reproduce existing structures and relations of power. Did my initial resistance to dominant gender roles in naming myself an 'activist' function to reinforce the patriarchal mapping of the world? Embracing the term 'activist', do I collude with the division of the world into 'active' and 'passive', male and female, public and private?[1] Perhaps it is the case, as Gilbert and Gubar (1979) suggest, that women find it necessary to act out male metaphors, as if trying to understand their implications. The 'trying on' of masculinist narratives such as 'activist' speaks to the disruption of a stable coherent self while simultaneously serving to warn us that because 'narrative conventions work as unconscious ideologies on individual subjects, patriarchal and other harmful ideologies are often represented, produced, and reworked in the texts and stories women write and tell, thus causing them to participate in their own oppression' (Bloom and Munro 1995:25).

What had not initially been apparent to me was that my idealization of resistance reproduced the masculinist narrative of the autonomous individual and, in effect, reproduced the modes of oppression that I sought to criticize. My romanticized view of resistance, as embedded in the individual, actually served to reify the fiction of a unitary, stable and coherent subject. So, in the end I did not 'give voice' to stories of resistance as I originally understood the term. Instead, by focusing on the personal narratives in the life histories of women teachers, how and why they tell their stories, as well as what they tell becomes significant in understanding forms of resistance. It was the life historians' resistance to traditional notions of power, manifested in the continual construction of their subjectivity, which attuned me to the complex and contradictory ways in which women resist gender norms and name their agency.

In the end, it was not the challenge of fitting these women's stories into dominant theoretical constructs that proved profound, but the stories themselves, which embodied the agency of self-representation. The stories revealed the limits of dominant notions of subjectivity, agency and resistance. I did not find teachers who called themselves subversives. I did not hear tales of revolution, but instead the stories of women who, through the act of teaching, embodied their vision of a more just society. It was the telling of the stories, the act of naming oneself, that was powerful, for it revealed the agency we have in constructing and shaping our lives despite the roles prescribed for women.

In this chapter, I review the forms of self-representation engaged by the three life historians and examine the implications for critical and poststructuralist theories of resistance, power and knowledge, and subjectivity. My claim is that women's resistance has not been recognized as such when it has been written against the dominant representations of identity and authority as masculine. In rethinking resistance it is most important that we set aside normative assumptions of what constitutes resistance and agency by taking seriously women teachers' lives as a site for theorizing concepts such as resistance, agency and subjectivity. Like Leigh Gilmore (1994:12), I hope to analyse how women use 'self-representation and its constitutive possibilities for agency and subjectivity to become subjects . . . who exchange the position of object for the subjectivity of self-representational agency'.

Self-representation occurs within and through the discourses made available to us. Thus, my focus in this final chapter is on how and when women take up particular subject positions and how this attunes us to the dynamics of power relations. I turn my attention specifically to how these women rewrite their lives against and within the discourses of teaching as 'women's true profession' and 'professionalization' and within the discourse of regulation. Embedded in the narratives of Agnes, Cleo and Bonnie are each woman's efforts to create and shape reality in keeping with her self-image in the face of societal expectations that impose on women prescribed scripts of gendered norms. The tension between societal norms and the creation of our own stories reveals our struggle, not only within ourselves, but with the social world. When subjectivity is understood as a dynamic process, rather than a fixed concept, how these women write their lives constitutes new understandings of power and agency. They rewrite resistance.

Rewriting the discourse of teaching as 'women's true profession'

A central theme throughout the life history narratives were the stories of 'becoming teachers'. The women described themselves as committed to education, so I assumed I would hear stories about women who entered teaching consciously so as to bring about change. I did not expect to hear the stories of resistance they told about entering teaching. Yet, each of the life historians struggled in some way with her decision to enter the teaching profession despite the gendered norm that teaching was 'women's true profession'. As I sought to understand what I perceived as a contradiction in their life-long commitment to education and their resistance to entering teaching, I recognized that this not only represented a site of gender conflict, but that in coming up against gender ideologies that conflicted with their own understandings of self, this was a site of resistance.

Teaching served as a space in which these women continually defined themselves by reconciling conflicting images of self and societal expectations. For each of them, taking up the identity of teacher was fraught with tensions as a result of the deeply gendered discourse of teaching as women's true profession. Not only does this discourse maintain an essentialized nature of gender, thus precluding agency, but in being perceived as a woman's profession, teaching is devalued. To enter into a profession that is not only devalued, but that suggests women do not have agency, is to participate in a form of self-erasure. To take up an identity as a teacher, without erasing one's self, requires a complex negotiation. It is this negotiation, as a form of agency, that has been obscured when women's motivations for entering teaching have been attributed to women's natural proclivities.

Consequently, despite the stereotype that women go into teaching because they love children, not one of the women gave this as a reason for entering the field.[2] The stories told reveal many motives and desires for entering teaching, including issues related to class, gender, place and historic period. Agnes tells the story that 'she didn't think of teaching at all', although she simultaneously maintains that teaching was the only profession open to women. Cleo claims she 'stumbled' into teaching and went into it because all her friends were teachers. Bonnie suggests that teaching was what everyone was doing and that there 'weren't many alternatives'. In making these claims, these women contest the essentializing gender expectations embedded in the discourse of teaching as women's true profession. As Leigh Gilmore (1994) has suggested, in not being able to identify with a category, in this case the dominant representations of women teachers, agency becomes possible. Their self-representations position them outside dominant gender ideologies and thus they can deflect these and do not have to be defined by them.

In addition to these key phrases, several patterns became obvious to me in their narratives of becoming teachers. First was their deferral of their decision to enter teaching to others: Bonnie claims she went into teaching because 'that's what everybody else was doing'; Agnes claims they 'rarely went into anything else'; and Cleo claims she went into teaching 'because all my friends were doing it'. This deferral signified to me the discomfort they experienced in taking up an identity as a teacher.[3] From my perspective, actively choosing to become teachers would have been tantamount to subscribing to the essentialized gender norms embedded in the discourse of teaching as women's true profession.

And yet, their deferral did not conform to my notions of agency and resistance. Instead their narratives of deferral, in which they in effect give up their agency, was reminiscent of the expectations that women be passive, 'dutiful daughters'. Their deferral of agency functioned on one level as compliance with the ideology of teaching as women's true profession. What I perceived as an oppressive ideology, which situated women in an essentializing discourse, was reappropriated by these women to reconcile their conflicted feelings on entering the teaching profession. Although they initially resist the discourse of teaching as women's true profession, and position themselves outside it, they must ultimately justify their decision to enter teaching. Ironically, they appropriate the ideology of teaching as women's true profession to legitimate their decision to enter teaching. However, in appropriating it, they make it their own and thus deflect the essentializing nature of the discourse. The simultaneous rejection and appropriation of this ideology functions not only to displace gender norms but to keep in flux the effects of this discourse as a means of displacing it.

Ironically, resistance, traditionally understood as the rejection of dominant ideologies, in this case was constituted by embracing the hegemonic ideologies of teaching as 'women's true profession'. Engaging the dominant ideology enabled them to reconcile their decision to enter teaching in spite of conflicting family expectations or self-images. Engaging the dominant ideology provides an alternative to critical and neo-Marxist conceptions of resistance as opposition to dominant ideologies to bring about change. Here the traditional notion of critical and neo-Marxist theorists that insists on rejection of mainstream ideologies to create change excludes the women invoking dominant ideologies to create the conditions in which they felt they could become teachers and work for social change.

A second pattern that emerged in the narratives of becoming teachers was telling the story that they entered teaching because it was the only profession open to women, although clerical, nursing and other professions were also open to women. Why is it necessary to tell this story? Like deferring their decisions to others, telling this fiction allows them to take up a teacher identity while maintaining their own self-understanding as powerful and as active agents. This fiction suggesting that no other professions were open to women creates a reality that allows them to enter teaching without erasing their agency. In other words, despite going into teaching (as essentialized discourse) they can still construct a self-image as an active subject because they had no other choices. In essence they reify the discourse of teaching as women's true profession while simultaneously disrupting it through their telling of a fiction.

If we could not imagine our roles as teachers beyond the dominant stereotypes written for women, what desire would there be for many women to become teachers? In redefining their lives through stories, real and imagined, I believe we resist the naming of our experiences by others' definitions of what reality should or ought to be. In contesting the patriarchal scripts written for women, we reconstruct history to fit our understandings of our experiences, despite dominant assumptions that teaching is natural and not an active extension of our lives. Thus, our constructions, our fictions, express the visions we hope or wish to enact. Trinh Minh-ha (1991:8) suggests that 'our very existence consists in our imagination of ourselves'. The fictions that women write about teaching, the engagement of imagination to write and rewrite our lives, consequently becomes one source of resistance in enacting our own lives. These sites of struggle provide profound spaces in which to explore the conflicting discourses and power relationships with which women grapple in their struggle to make their lives real.

Rewriting the discourse of professionalization

The discourse of professionalism has functioned in contradictory ways to shape women's subjectivity. On the one hand, Agnes takes up the discourse of professionalism as a means to deflect the devaluation of teaching because it is 'women's work'. At the same time, the image of the professional as gender neutral and objective has legitimized the regulation of women teachers, in particular their bodies. I am reminded of my own 'trying on' of professionalism as a means to legitimate my decision to enter teaching. There is nothing inherently oppressive or liberatory about the discourse of professionalization. It is how, when and why women take up this discourse that suggests how gender norms are inscribed in power relationships.

The professionalization of teaching is a discourse that spans the current century and has taken on a variety of meanings. In other words, it has not always constructed representations of teachers in the same ways; it has been used in conflicting ways. The committed, single teacher who devoted her life to teaching, was not seen as a professional in the 1920s and 1930s, but as a spinster. The woman teacher as professional was caricatured as abnormal, asexual or homosexual; as unfeminine. Thus, what constitutes 'professionalism' is not static but is central to the construction of and production of gender ideologies. How the women teachers in this study negotiate the often contradictory subjectivities made available to them suggests that these ideologies are not imposed and do not function as hegemonic.

Women's self-representational acts in relation to the discourse of professionalism are the focus of this section. Professionalization privileges autonomy, hierarchy and segmentation. I attend specifically to one aspect of professionalism; the assumption that a profession is marked by a sequence of stages that denote hierarchy and advancement. In teaching this has meant that commitment and degree of professionalism has been measured by one's advancement into administration. What I suggest in this section is that the norms embedded in this view of teaching regarding what is a career, success and commitment do not adequately describe the experiences of the women teachers in this study. I saw this happening in several ways. The most obvious was that the teachers did not speak of their teaching careers in terms of beginning or end but rather as fluid and continual. Teaching is neither confined to the years in which one formally worked nor limited to the corporate model of a career, which bases success and commitment on a hierarchical model of advancement up the career ladder.

The lack of a long-term, planned career has often been interpreted as evidence of women's lack of commitment to work. Historically teachers have been perceived as working only for 'pin' money or traversing dual responsibilities of teaching and family, resulting in an image of women teachers as careerless, and thus not professionals (Lortie 1975). Sari Biklen (1983) has challenged this interpretation by claiming that although womens' lives do not fit the 'corporate' model on which men's careers have been studied this does not mean they are not committed. While others (Lortie 1975) suggest that women's 'flat career lines' reflect a lack of agency and are evidence of women's lack of commitment to work, this work suggests that teachers' decisions regarding professional behaviour reflect a different set of values.

This was particularly evident in the stories of administration. Originally, my goal had been to work with women teachers. I had no intention of exploring women in administration. Although the three life historians I worked with were introduced to me as 'teachers', it turned out that each of them had also been an administrator. Initially, I interpreted their moves into administration as a form of resistance on two levels. First, moving into administration contested dominant understandings of women teachers as having a low work commitment. Second, I saw their moves into administration as their taking on positions of power from which they could enact change. In hindsight, my original interpretations were embedded within understandings of change as consolidation of power and as a progressive series of incremental moves within a hierarchy of power. Again, what I interpreted as resistance, the life historians named something else. In the following sections I explore how these women negotiated the discourse of professionalism as reflected in their moves into administration, a male subject position, while maintaining their own self-representations.

Naming it teaching: resisting moving 'up' the career ladder

Despite career norms that suggest that moving into administration is a step up the ladder, and is central to measuring one's success, the women not only deferred their moves into administration to others but, in some cases, as Biklen (1983) has described, women teachers saw moving 'up' into administration as diminishing the quality of their work as educators and thus actually resisted becoming administrators. According to Biklen's (1983) study of elementary school educators, many teachers base their decision not to 'advance' in their careers on the belief that the quality of their work as educators of children would suffer. They did not view moving to an administrative position as a 'step up' the career ladder; instead, it was a step away from students. In effect, their sense of agency in staying teachers acts as a form of resistance against hierarchical, patriarchal notions of success embedded in the discourse of professionalism.

For the women in this study who chose to move into administration the decision was no less problematic. They revealed discomfort in what they experienced as a betrayal of their students and in assuming a position of public authority usually reserved for males. To some degree, each of these women was reluctant to become an administrator. Cleo and Bonnie repeatedly attributed their moves to others, and primarily to male administrators. I perceived this as a way to ease their conflicting feelings at leaving the classroom yet still maintaining their identity as teachers.

The conflict for those women who became administrators, I believe, was that their motives would be judged by normative expectations for female behaviour, which suggest that women are powerless and lack authority. Thus, in becoming administrators they crossed gender boundaries, taking up positions usually reserved for men. When administration signifies a male subject position and teacher signifies a female subject position the gender negotiation that must take place in order for women to assume what has traditionally been defined as a male position is tricky at best. The primary way I saw them negotiate this gender conflict was by adamantly choosing to identify themselves as teachers rather than as administrators. Cleo recalled,

> Teachers were always good to me. I had very few situations where they were out to get me, which is not too abnormal with administrators. I'm still with teacher groups. I am not with administrators. I'm with the same group of women as when we started and most of us were teaching. Now we're all retired. But they're all teachers. Classroom teachers. Once a month we all have dinner or something.

Naming themselves teachers, despite the fact that they worked as administrators, functions as resistance on two levels. First, women reject the shaping of their lives according to male norms and expectations by speaking in the language of teaching, which subverts hierarchy. The women administrators use the naming of themselves as teachers to assert the intentionality that teachers have. They reinvest the authority usually given to administrators, a traditionally male domain, back into teachers, whose authority is often questioned by administrators. By refusing to call themselves administrators, they resist a notion of control and power that does not conform to their understandings of change as embedded in relationships rather than imposed from an authority position. Second, in refusing to name themselves administrators and in reconceptualizing their careers so that they are not bracketed by the usual career norms of the corporate model, these women rewrite their lives to fit their experiences. In essence, women teachers resist traditional notions of career, success and commitment, which separate, dichotomize and establish hierarchical levels. By naming themselves teachers, these women deflect career norms based on men's understandings, which do not reflect the meanings they give to their work.

The writings of Mikhail Bakhtin (1981) suggest that those who wish to speak about forbidden topics – in this case, the personal and subjective experiences of women – must resort to various forms of verbal subterfuge to communicate with one another. Creating alternatives to standard forms of language becomes a form of resistance. I saw these teachers resolve their conflicting feelings through engaging in 'verbal subterfuge' through the naming of themselves as teachers, not administrators. By subverting the system, by speaking in a language which is not acknowledged and rarely understood, these women deflected patriarchal career norms and definitions of teaching. Women whose use of the master's language would result only in their being trapped in the master's game (Lorde 1984) have created alternatives to standard forms of language that serve as resistance. In 'naming it teaching' these women teachers resist the fixing of one's career to an abstract plotting of career progress along coordinates of success, based on climbing the career ladder as a measure of professionalism, which does not speak to their own personal motivations, values and experiences.

Deferral as resistance

As mentioned earlier, I interpreted their moves up the 'career ladder' into administration as a form of resistance in which they located themselves in positions of power usually reserved for males and, more importantly, from which they could enact change. I was intrigued by their stories of becoming administrators because it disrupted the stereotype of women teachers as lacking motivation and career aspirations and spoke to my understanding of teachers as activists. Again, what I interpreted as resistance, they named something else. For example, Cleo reflected on her position as district coordinator of curriculum, 'It was something I did; it wasn't that I wanted to move to some other plateau . . . I wasn't trying to reach the top in either teaching or administration; I had no desire to be the top Joe.' Cleo and Bonnie's attributing their career achievements to others as well as their consistent stories of discomfort in becoming administrators seemed again to highlight the tension between my reading of their stories as willing 'daughters' to patriarchy's desired subservience and their decentralizing of traditional masculinist norms through resisting 'moves up' the career ladder.

Cleo and Bonnie repeatedly attributed their moves to others and primarily to male administrators. Cleo made it clear regarding her position as social studies curriculum coordinator; 'I didn't apply for it, I was asked'. Bonnie recalled, 'I ended up involved in activities where male administrators gave me a lot of positive encouragement'. Attributing their career moves to others seemed to be one way in which they eased their conflicting feelings at leaving the classroom and their discomfort in taking up a masculinist 'ambition–career' plot. Ironically, the narrative strategy of deferral acts as a form of agency when it allows them to position themselves in a subject position usually reserved for men. Because this strategy works to simultaneously reify and resist gender norms, I would maintain that these women subvert an either/or notion of gender as a binary. In other words, they do not give up a female subject position for a male subject position. This type of negotiation would merely reinforce gender binaries of male and female unitary subject positions. It is the simultaneous rejection and reappropriation achieved through the strategy of deferral that disrupts the power of the discourse of professionalization.

The drifter

In light of their successful careers and what I perceived as an orderly progression, in most cases from teacher through chairperson to administrator, I was surprised at the manner in which Agnes, Cleo and Bonnie described their careers as 'not planned'. In speaking about their work, the women often described their careers as 'just happening', or it was an 'accident' or 'I was lucky'. Cleo recalled moving into administration; 'I just sort of fell into it' and 'I was a drifter'. I struggled to understand why they 'resisted' conceptualizing themselves as active agents. Had they internalized patriarchal norms so well that they were merely acting out their roles as 'dutiful and appropriately meek daughters'? (Jacobs 1992).

In recalling their professional lives, they chose not to describe their careers based on the corporate model as a planned progression of career moves. What might be interpreted as a lack of commitment or motivation by some, I interpreted as an expression of resistance in which they defined themselves outside the traditional norms and expectations by envisaging themselves as drifters. Again, resistance – in this case to acknowledging their own agency in becoming administrators – was in opposition to my search for resistance as counterhegemonic. I struggled to understand what I saw as a contradiction.

Cleo's image of herself as a drifter was particularly problematic because of her apparently strong sense of self and conviction. Cleo's story intrigued me because of what I perceived to be the contradictions between her role as district administrator and her persistent claims that 'she never wanted to be the top Joe'. She reflected on her career, 'It wasn't conscious. I didn't plan ahead. I was a drifter.' Her description of herself as a drifter contrasted strongly with my own perception of Cleo as actively pursuing a career despite societal norms that she described as, 'I think you were expected to get married and have a family'. I wondered why, despite her success, she persisted throughout our interviews to attribute her success to others or to chance. I wondered, did her image of herself as a 'drifter' allow her to construct a self that fit more readily with social expectations of women as powerless and without authoritative roles? Or was it, as Carolyn Heilbrun (1988) has pointed out, that women have difficulty taking credit for their accomplishments because they see these as grounded in relation to others, not as individual, autonomous accomplishments.

At first, I did not interpret Cleo's story of the 'drifter' as a form of resistance. Again, my understandings of resistance and change, which assumed that change results from deliberate and active resistance to the structures perpetuating oppression seemed to get in the way. Until now, my understandings of resistance and change, shaped by a critical and neo-Marxist perspective, assumed that change was oppositional, intentional and public. Yet, paradoxically, Cleo's lack of intentionality, through the naming of herself as a drifter, becomes transformed into an expression of agency. By seeing herself outside societal norms, she deflects and decentres these and does not have to be defined by them. In this sense, the drifter can write her own script. Revisioning her life as that of a 'drifter', Cleo displaced patriarchal norms, allowing her to write her own story. bell hooks (1990:145) suggests that it is from the margins that we can 'envision new alternatives, oppositional aesthetic acts'.

Bettina Aptheker (1989:171) maintains that traditional understandings of resistance assume that change is 'social rather than individual, political rather than personal, and that resistance implies a movement embracing large numbers of people in conscious alliance for a common goal'. In listening to these women's stories, new understandings of resistance were emerging, which highlighted the complex interactions of women's struggle to make their lives real. Reconceptualizing resistance as grounded in women's ability to displace traditional gender norms through metaphors like the 'drifter' and to disrupt dominant ideologies through engaging them seemed to capture my understanding of poststructuralist conceptions of power.

Yet, despite my understanding of poststructuralist (Foucault 1979) perspectives as acknowledging power relations as situated, shifting and fragmented, I wondered why I had had such difficulty in recognizing and naming these forms of resistance, which now seemed so clear. The life historians' understandings of themselves as drifters, as outsiders, highlighted the fact that women are situated differently within power relationships (Bartky 1990; Hartstock 1990). As Cleo often commented, 'I resisted, I didn't try to change things' or 'I really didn't fight it; a fight with no chance of winning is not a real good fight'. As Sandra Bartky (1990) suggests, Foucault's understanding of social relationships neglects the fact that women are situated differently within power relationships. Excluded from the construction of dominant social theories, as well as the resultant norms, women function as outsiders in the system of relationships as Foucault describes them. For women who explicitly or implicitly understand their 'otherness' and seek to maintain their identity, survival depends on displacing dominant social relationships through metaphors like the drifter or the narrative of deferral.

These women's constructions of knowledge of themselves is a reflection of power relationships. In situating themselves outside dominant social relations as drifters, their constructions of themselves become a form of empowerment. I agree with Carolyn Heilbrun (1988:18) that power is the ability to take one's place in whatever discourse is essential to action. For some women, this has been in the margins (hooks 1990). I am reminded of Charlotte Perkins Gilman's (1981) conclusion in her short story *The Yellow Wallpaper*, her fictionalized autobiographical account of her struggle to stay real as she peels back the layers of wallpaper in the room where she has been confined by her husband. At the end of the story, she declares, 'I've got out at last . . . And I've pulled off most of the paper, so you can't put me back!'. Escaping the roles prescribed for women (even through madness), the metaphorical use of wallpaper for the patriarchal scripts written to contain women, identity and thus survival, becomes embodied in the continual peeling back or traversing of these boundaries.

By resisting a stable, coherent self, the metaphor of the drifter provides a continual displacement through which these women resist the naming of their realities by others. The displacement of the unitary subject becomes a form of resistance in which power is dispersed rather than consolidated. In rewriting the discourse of professionalism this displacement and dispersal functions as a form of resistance to the masculinist norms embedded in the discourse of professionalism. In particular the use of the drifter suggests that gender is constructed not as professional (male) or non-professional (female) but through and in a continual crossing of gender boundaries, which results in a decentring of the gender binary creating spaces from which to envisage a multiplicity of genders.

Rewriting the discourse of regulation

The woman teacher has been the site of the control and regulation of gender norms.[4] This regulation ranges from overt 'laws' or rules, which prohibited certain behaviours, like marriage, to less apparent, but no less powerful, forms of regulation, like the self-regulation or policing that women participate in. What these types of regulation have in common is that they focus on the body as a medium of social control. The definition and shaping of the body is the focal point for struggles over the shape of power. Women have not been docile subjects of this inscription.[5] The life history narratives presented in this work present several examples of how women 'resist' the regulation of their bodies, as well as how this resistance challenges dominant concepts of subjectivity as unitary.

I begin with Agnes and her decision not to marry. Agnes claims she 'didn't have to marry' and thus signals her choice to reject the marriage plot. When marriage signifies normal female behaviour and desires, the decision not to marry suggests a rejection of normative femininity. Agnes exchanges the pattern of marriage for a life of meaningful work with students and colleagues, whom she names as her family. In rewriting the family outside the confines of the 'nuclear family' Agnes constructs her own vision of female subjectivity. Although the appropriation of the family metaphor suggests the power of this discourse to work on and shape our understandings of self and thus might be interpreted as compliance with dominant norms, I maintain that Agnes's exchange of the nuclear family for a family of her own choosing functions as a form of resistance to the regulation of female bodies through marriage. Agnes was in fact part of a larger community of single women educators who were engaged in redefining gender norms on a daily basis by creating alternative lifestyles (settlement houses, Boston marriages, women's colleges) that rejected the marriage plot. These alternatives provided spaces that not only rewrote public culture but allowed for women to be embodied through rewriting the cultural norms of femininity.

This reshaping of the public sphere did not go unchallenged and once again the body is the site of regulation that attempts to put women in their place. It is no accident that the image of the spinster emerged precisely when large numbers of women were actively seeking to be independent and creating institutions that would sustain that independence. The image of the spinster – the single woman teacher – suggests abnormality; a pathology of not being feminine. The gender neutral representations embedded in the image of the spinster suggest that a woman is acting like a man. How this stereotype functions on an unconscious level to regulate women teachers' behaviour through dress and demeanour can only be projected. What is clear in Agnes's narrative is that she had to negotiate binary gender norms with her own subjective understandings. Agnes's narrative suggests that in negotiating female subjectivity she believed one could 'think like a man' and 'be feminine'. In essence she is suggesting that women can be both male and female. In rejecting an either/or concept of gender she resists the duality and finality of unitary concepts of gender identity. Leigh Gilmore (1994:140) suggests that when women can envisage themselves outside two positions of gender difference, which inevitably represent her as either 'unrepresentable' or 'repressed' in phallic discourse, then women regain 'revisionary leverage against the cultural roles prescribed in marriage'. Rejecting an either/or dilemma of gender resists a naturalized reading of bodies in which sexual difference is a given.

The ongoing power of the marriage plot, despite the supposed 'liberation' movement, is evidenced in Bonnie's narrative. Bonnie recalled about her first marriage, 'I think I got married to be respectable as a teacher'. The assumption is that single women are not respectable; they do not conform to gender norms. Like Agnes she rewrites the marriage plot by maintaining that after her first marriage she was, 'trying to create something separate and distinct'. She continued by saying, 'I chose not to have children. I could never envision myself with children. I always had all these other things to do.' In claiming her agency she resists the power of the dominant marriage plot to regulate her life.

Cleo's reflections that, 'I think you were supposed to get married' also signal her disruption of the hegemony of the marriage plot. For Cleo, who did marry and have children, this resistance to understanding the dominant expectations for women suggests that she was not merely acquiescing to gender norms. What is notable is that Cleo never discussed her husband or son in our interviews. When I asked about family she replied, 'you don't want to know about that, it doesn't have anything to do with my work'. In this sense Cleo complies with the separation of public and private. As Elizabeth Hancock (1989:29) points out, to be taken seriously 'at work' one must keep private concerns out of the public arena. Her body, her sexuality and capacity to bear children are in essence hidden from public view.

How the marriage plot is intertwined with representations of teachers as a means of regulating the female body is rarely discussed in relation to women teachers' lives and their work. More importantly, how these women deflect this plot suggests forms of resistance that embody a decentralizing of unitary conceptions of gender. Additionally, the various ways in which femininity is taken up suggest the fluid nature of gender ideologies between and across time and across micro- and macrolevels.

Docile bodies as resistant bodies[6]

Traditionally, the body is seen, by feminists, as a site of oppression. Accordingly, it also becomes the potential focus of liberation. Liberation means control of the body by women, rather than men. This subversion, however, maintains binary concepts of gender, which then reproduces the male and female body as natural. Judith Butler (1990) maintains that positing a strong or autonomous female subject leaves intact gender bipolarities and institutional structures that support given gender positions. More importantly, it retains notions of power as a source of liberation. My question is, how can we theorize docile bodies? If the strong woman is complicit, what about the woman who appears to perform femininity according to the rules? Judith Butler (1990) has suggested that the 'performance of femininity' in effect functions as a mocking enactment of gender, and thus exposes and subverts the notion of true gender identity. When performance of femininity is equated with compliance to gender norms the complex ways in which power and resistance circulate remain obscured.

I think here particularly of Bonnie, whose narrative contains the most obvious examples of the regulation of the body. Bonnie's story of her principal admonishing her for wearing sandals functions as a form of regulation. Her feet, symbolic of her femininity, must be contained, covered and kept out of sight. Ironically, Bonnie is perceived by her principal to be too feminine, not 'professional' enough; in other words, not male enough. The presence of her femaleness is in contrast to the dominant norms, which code the public sphere as male. For Bonnie this regulation was also experienced in her VISTA experience through accusations that she was being 'unwittingly seductive'. The telling of her stories of the accusation of being unwittingly seductive and of the reprimand for wearing sandals suggests that the regulation of her body was central to her understandings of self. Naming these experiences is, on one level, an act of agency, in that she makes them real despite her initial confusion that she 'couldn't really get what they were getting at'. Her state of disbelief signifies her own reading of her body against dominant representations and norms. And yet, her state of disbelief also functions to ignore the 'reality' of her experience. This can't be real, thus oppression of this nature doesn't really exist. Bonnie functions as a docile body. Ironically, this denial allows Bonnie to retain a self-representation as powerful. As Susan Bordo (1993:192) points out, 'our very docility can have consequences that are personally liberating and/or culturally transforming'.

What is resistance to one person may be seen as submission to another. Many poststructuralist feminists have argued that overt forms of power are not necessary to maintain docile female bodies. We police our own bodies. We turn the male gaze on ourselves, thereby complying with socially sanctioned norms of behaviour. I suggest that Bonnie's narrative rejects this hegemonic reading of self-regulation. Although Bonnie complies to gender norms, this situates her in a position from which she can act without the ongoing regulation of the male gaze. Thus self-regulation can be interpreted as accommodation and resistance. In accommodating, in performing femininity, women can deflect the heightened attention and thus regulation of the male gaze.[7]

However, what must be remembered is that women's bodies are the site through which attempts to maintain gendered norms are carried out. That this is central to women teachers' experiencing of their subjectivity and how they negotiate their understandings of themselves as teachers has been ignored. Rather than leave us frustrated, I think these complexities highlight the continual disruption of gender relations and warn against simplistic analysis of gendered or other ideologies.

Reconstructing gender, subjectivity and resistance

I do not mean to romanticize the lives of women teachers or to suggest a monolithic view of women teachers as resistors. Yet, in today's postmodern world I walk a fine line. For as women, if we explore our agency or claim our own voices, we are reminded of the potential totalizing tendencies of asserting a stable and coherent identity. Yet, if we abandon our search do we risk complying with patriarchy's aim to name our desires?

In working with these women I hoped to gain a better understanding of how women teachers experience their gendered positions and the consequent shaping of their understandings of teaching. I was caught off guard when gender did not emerge as a central theme in the interviews. The women I interviewed never made explicit reference to it. I was confused by what I perceived as the contradictory statements of women who insisted that 'being a woman never made a difference' or that 'they never thought about being a woman', and the stories in which they described themselves as being treated unfairly. It then occurred to me that gender is such an implicit part of our lives, that we often take it for granted. 'You wake up every day meeting the gender question, so you don't even notice it' (Bateson 1989:44).

The experiences of Agnes, Cleo and Bonnie suggest that women's experiences of gender are multiple, situated and contradictory. Their stories illuminate the multiple experiences of teachers; the various ways in which gender ideologies are contested and invoked in shaping our identities. Despite the multiple and contradictory definitions of our female subjectivity, I do not believe that this precludes agency or resistance. The fact that these women take a daily position in shaping and creating their identities, through the various ways identified above, reflects an acknowledgement of the continual process of defining and redefining our self-images and identities in the light of many contextual considerations. The situated and often contradictory nature of gender relations speaks to the various ways in which these women experience their gendered selves across time and space, and sheds light on my understanding of them. The narrative strategies these women engage – appropriating dominant ideologies, constructing fictions, verbal subterfuge, deferral, defining themselves as drifters and being docile bodies – suggest complex and contradictory forms of resistance. Each of these strategies functions as a means to resist the duality and finality of gender. In keeping their subject positions continually in flux these strategies for self-representation function, according to Leigh Gilmore (1994:133) to 'narrativize gender less as an inevitable identity than as a focus for self-representational agency'. Thus agency is not bound to 'a' subject position but in the ongoing resistance to any stable and unitary identity.

Ultimately, these women's narratives reveal the limits of dominant notions of identity. In keeping their gendered subjectivity in flux, as positioned both inside and outside the ideology of gender, the narratives reflect de Lauretis (1984) theory of the 'female-gendered subject' who 'recognizes and knows herself, to some extent, through her culture's gender codes but who can also critique this coding and read gender as a construction' (Gilmore 1994:20). According to Gilmore (1995:20),

> the 'feminine' subject immersed in the ideology of gender is not the only gendered construction available to women. Indeed, the various positionings of women within and against constructions of gender provides a powerful illustration for claims against the 'naturalness' of gender.

The ongoing negotiation of gendered subjectivity evident in the life history narratives presented here suggests that women's experiencing of gender is not monolithic or grounded in understandings of gender as inevitable. In continually becoming, in naming and renaming, in moving back and forth into the margins, women actively subvert and decentralize dominant relationships. Resistance becomes a never-ending dance in these spaces of contradiction. Consequently, as I learned from Agnes, Cleo and Bonnie, resistance is not an 'act' but a movement, a continual displacement of others' attempts to name our realities. This is a resistance born out of survival, an attempt to stay real and claim the realities of our lives as women, as teachers and as women who choose to be teachers.

Notes

1 I would like to acknowledge Geraldine Clifford for pointing this out to me in the course of our correspondence.
2 Biklen (1995) also portrays the conflicts women experienced in becoming teachers.
3 See also Jacobs *et al.* (1995) for a discussion of the role of deferral in women teachers' lives.
4 Biklen (1995) also uses the 'discourses of regulation' as a framework for analysis.
5 As Bordo (1993:193) maintains, 'the dominant discourses of femininity are continually allowing for the eruption of "difference", and even the most subordinated subjects are therefore continually confronted with opportunities for resistance, for making meanings that oppose or evade the dominant ideology'.
6 See Kohli (1996) for a further discussion of 'docile' bodies.
7 See Ropers-Huilman (1998), in particular the chapter 'Multiplicity in action: Working through identities', which provides numerous examples of how teachers consciously construct their appearance in compliance with dominant norms of femininity to help establish and maintain their authority.

Epilogue

My original desire to conduct collaborative, reflexive research which would acknowledge the intersubjective process of meaning making was in reality quite a different story. This chapter, based on field notes and discussions with the life historians on the process of conducting life history inquiry, deconstructs that process.

Imposing collaboration

Feminists have been particularly sensitive to seeking alternatives to the traditional, hierarchical research relationship which they see as potentially exploitative, and a reification of patriarchal power relationships (Lather 1986; Christman 1988; Stacey 1988). Ethnographic research, due to its focus on understanding the insider's or emic meaning, has shifted the traditional focus of power from the researcher to the researched. Agar's (1980) notion of the informant as 'one up', inverts the traditional hierarchy by creating the subject as expert, although the dualisms and dichotomy of the research relationship are still maintained. In this study I sought to avoid the alienation between the researcher and researched that results from this subject–object polarity (Gitlin 1990).

Like others engaged in collaborative research, I hoped to establish an egalitarian, reciprocal relationship, which acknowledged the mutual and two-way nature of the research relationship (Golde 1970; Reinharz 1979; Duelli-Klein 1983; Robertson 1983). The informant is not a passive, objectified function of data, nor the insider on whom the researcher is dependent for insight. Both the researcher and researched are active participants in the research relationship and knowledge is viewed as socially and intersubjectively constructed.

One way in which I hoped to acknowledge the collaborative nature of the research relationship was by having each of the life historians keep a personal journal of their reactions to our ongoing work together. In addition to engaging them in the research through reflective writing, I hoped the journals would provide me with an understanding of the intersubjective nature of the research process. Despite what I thought were my well intentioned goals, both of the central participants rejected this suggestion, saying I could ask them questions, but they did not wish to write independently.

My first attempt at establishing a collaborative relationship was flatly rejected. I sensed that my request was perceived as a demand that did not conform to my participants' conceptualization of the research process. My heightened sensitivity to avoiding an exploitative research relationship had not taken into account the fact that my participants had their own reasons and agendas for participating in the study. In essence, my assumption of the need for a collaborative relationship underlined my perception of them as disempowered, thereby disregarding their power to determine the nature of the relationship.

My focus on collaboration had not taken into account that the life historians would develop their own framing of our relationship. When I arrived at Cleo's home for our first interview she was in the process of preparing coffee and warming freshly baked bread. She commented, 'I thought about using my good china, but then decided that this was work and settled on using the everyday dishes'. Bonnie, answering the phone during one of our interviews, replied that she was working and would have to get back to the caller later. For these women, we were not engaged in chatter between friends, but in serious work. These incidents highlighted for me the multiple meanings that the participants created for understanding their role in the research process. What I thought would be enjoyable talk, they thought of as work. I was now faced with understanding the implications of their positioning themselves in a working relationship. Did they see themselves as co-workers, employer and employee or as colleagues? Perhaps more importantly, how did they define work? What did work mean to them? What was the importance of their categorizing our relationship as work? What implications did this have in reconceptualizing the roles and responsibilities of both the researcher and researched? These questions made clear the negotiated and constructed nature of the research relationship.

In establishing a collaborative relationship I believed I would also share my story. I engaged in life history research because of its reciprocal nature involving mutual storytelling (Connelly and Clandinin 1990). Connelly and Clandinin (1990:4) emphasize the importance of the mutual construction of the research relationship by warning the researcher to be 'aware of constructing a relationship in which both voices are heard'. This paradox of the researcher trying to construct a mutual relationship becomes particularly problematic when a life historian is not interested in hearing the researcher's story. Often when I spoke to Bonnie, telling her about myself, she seemed disinterested and looked confused as to why I should talk so much when I

was there to hear her story. Was I imposing my story on her? Was it to be
the case that as researcher I became objectified in my role as passive listener?
In attempting to construct a collaborative relationship, whose needs were
really being served?

I struggled to define the nature of our relationship. My own understanding of collaboration implied that the nature of the relationship be that of
friends. This conflicted with their perception of our relationship as work.
The businesslike nature of our relationships seemed at odds with my goal of
collaboration. My evolving understanding of Bonnie's and Cleo's framing of
our relationship as work led me to be cautious in being too friendly. If this
was a truly collaborative relationship, I felt the need to recognize and respect
their desire to maintain a working relationship.

I wondered whether my search for collaboration had turned into what
Marilyn Strathern (1987:290) calls 'a metaphor for an ideal ethical situation
in which neither voice is submerged by the Other'? Was collaboration a
delusion in which I could mask my discomfort with the hierarchical nature
of the research relationship by submerging our differences? Or, was the ultimate goal of the research process merely a selfish one designed to gain
understanding of myself by detour of the other? Strathern (1987) reminds us
that feminists traditionally are suspicious of the ethnographer's desire for
collaboration, a fear of being appropriated and spoken for. In my case, the
'other' was myself, and the fear that I would in some way misrepresent or
take advantage of them seemed to persist.

My efforts to establish collaboration seemed in vain. Was it to be, as
McRobbie (1982) and Stacey (1988) have suggested, that no matter how
hard we try to establish an egalitarian relationship, the research relationship
is inherently unequal and potentially exploitative and that, despite our
attempts to establish friendships, the perceived status and power differential
between the researcher and researched will always influence the research
relationship? These questions became particularly problematic as I
attempted to situate myself in the research and acknowledge the intersubjective nature of the research process.

Collaboration: getting 'too' close

Researchers engaged in ethnography or participant observation have long
revealed the dualistic and contradictory nature of the researcher–researched
relationship by discussing the emotional, as well as intellectual, complexities
of working in the field (Bowen 1964; Powdermaker 1966; Golde 1970;
Shostak 1981). Ethnographers engaged in close and long-term relationships
with 'informants', have stressed the delicate nature of the field relationship,
which demands openness and trust, even while it demands distance in order
to retain analytic competency (Everhart 1977). The researcher is warned not

to become too close to the 'subject' lest he or she lose the objectivity necessary for analysis.

Feminists engaged in ethnographic work have pointed out the exploitative
and unrealistic nature of pretending to be the 'objective' bystander (Stacey
1988; Abu-Lughod 1990; Roman and Apple 1990). The rejection of a grand
narrative, in light of the fact that realities are historically and culturally situated, has resulted in feminists pursuing subjectivity in order, as Abu-Lughod
(1990:15) puts it, to 'reclaim objectivity to mean precisely the situated view'.
In trying to be truly collaborative, I believed this meant not only acknowledging the subjective nature of the life historians' experiences, but also
revealing my own situated position.

There seemed to be a tension between the need to place myself in the
research process and the potential of revealing too much, thus predisposing
the participants to my analytic categories. Although I knew, in theory, that
notions of objectivity were false, I was afraid of imposing my analytic perspective by getting 'too' close. My goal was to understand how *they* perceived their lives as teachers. In some ways revealing too much about myself
seemed in conflict with my goal of using a life history methodology, which
would allow the life historian to speak for herself. I faced the contradiction
of wanting an open and honest relationship, and one that would allow me
to maintain the distance I felt I needed.

The tension between wanting to be open and honest, yet not predispose
the life historians to my biases, was problematic even before I began the
research process. I was cautioned that my strong feminist position might
'blind' me, causing me to see only what I wanted to see. I often wondered if
others conducting research were warned that they would focus too much on
class if they were Marxists, or too much on culture if they were ethnographers. Why was my predisposition any more dangerous? In contrast, I felt
that by openly acknowledging my subjectivity it would allow me to tap the
intersubjective process by 'attuning me to where self and subject are intertwined' (Peshkin 1988:20).

Women writing about other women (Chevigny 1984; Heilbrun 1988;
Bateson 1989) have described the process of understanding another
woman's life as one of empathy, identification and ultimately separation
with their informants. I sensed that without the process of identification,
difference could not be illuminated. The identification or connection, the
subjective experience I sought, seemed central to understanding them and
was necessary to write their life stories. These connections were however, in
part, dependent on my willingness to reveal my own story. Again, I wondered how much I should share?

I struggled. During the first interview and explanation of the project, I was
careful not to reveal too much. I was cautious not to identify myself as a
feminist, for fear that this might raise red flags or signal what I hoped to
hear. In the interviews I held back comments and my own experiences, and

tried to maintain neutral facial expressions so as not to lead them on or dispose them in any significant way. I wanted the themes to emerge from their stories. What role, if any, did they see gender playing in their lives as teachers? What meanings did they give to their lives as teachers? Would these stories emerge naturally if I told them too much? Like Kathy Anderson *et al.* (1990:120), I questioned if it was truly the life historian's understanding of her experience that I was seeking, or if I was structuring the interview so that the subject told the story that conformed to my orientation. Throughout the interviews it was difficult to listen without trying to make sense of the women's stories and place them within my theoretical framework. I often worried that this tendency was interfering with my ability to listen carefully to what the life historians were actually saying.

This was complicated by the fact that after the first interviews I tentatively identified three major themes. In the interviews that followed I felt my questions were guided by my need to gain a clearer understanding of these themes rather than allowing the participants to talk in a more open-ended manner. At the start of our fourth interview Bonnie mentioned that she wanted to talk about her travels, a significant part of her story which she felt she hadn't discussed. I, on the other hand, was anxious to hear more about what she had called her 'allies' and the role they played in her life as a female teacher. She deferred to my request, yet I wondered afterward how collaborative our interview had been.

In wanting to truly honour the voices of these women teachers, I faced another dilemma as I began supplementary interviews with former students, colleagues and administrators. My original intention was to conduct these interviews in an effort to enhance the subjective and contextual picture of the women I worked with. The life historians freely recommended people they believed would help me and who would be open to being interviewed. As I started these supplementary interviews, I began to question my own motives. When I asked Bonnie's principal to tell me the story of how Bonnie became division chair, I actually wanted to hear the other side of the story in order to identify incongruencies that might help me see the role gender played in Bonnie's school life. I also wondered how the principal's description of Bonnie would differ from her own or mine, hoping to gain more insight into Bonnie's own frame of reference.

These supplementary interviews were – and continue to be – very helpful in illuminating the subjective nature of our experiences, yet I wonder what role they have in a collaborative research relationship. I wonder if they undermine the purpose of feminist narrative inquiry, which seeks to validate women's voices and experiences as truth. Sheridan and Salaff (1984:17) maintain that,

> contradictory statements and actions are not necessarily false fronts that should be eliminated. On the contrary, sensitive recordings of

inconsistencies in what people say or do may show how perceptions of objective reality actually reflect different levels of more complex realities.

This notion of expanding subjectivity, increasing the reflexive process by holding 'reality' up to multiple mirrors certainly provides the opportunity to reflect the infinite and complex understandings of reality (Ruby 1982). However, I worry deeply about the potential loss of women's voices in this array of infinite possibilities. Does the pursuit of subjectivity lead us into the abyss of relativity? More importantly, can the collaboration of women and the findings of our research be acknowledged when all voices are equally valid?

Seeking subjectivity through collaboration continues to raise provoking questions. Although, I have not found a resolution to my continuing efforts to make sense of the research relationship, I am more cautious about naming the process collaborative or even suggesting that the research process can ever truly be collaborative. I say this especially in light of the fact that the research relationship in the field is only one aspect of the collaborative process. Genuine reciprocity entails not only sensitivity to the research relationship, but also an account of the research process and relationship in the final text. The problem of representation, of both the stories and the intersubjective process, presented me with my final dilemma.

'Where's my life in all of this?': collaboration and text

In trying to achieve a collaborative research relationship, the process and product of the research cannot be separated. In trying to recover the collaborative aspects of research in the text, the analysis and write-up has often been the exclusive concern of the researcher. According to Judith Stacey (1988:23) 'the lives, loves, and tragedies that field work informants share with a researcher are ultimately data, grist for the ethnographic mill, a mill that has a truly grinding power'. Leslie Roman (1989) points out that the ethnographer is written into the text, but rarely appears as a social subject in relation to those that she or he researches. An accounting of the relationship, its dynamics, its role in achieving understanding are traditionally left out due to their subjective nature. Feminists (Mies 1983; Harding 1989; Anderson et al. 1990) have warned against the dangers of de-materializing research accounts by stripping them of the economic, cultural and political conditions under which fieldwork has been conducted.

In seeking to establish a collaborative text, I was concerned not only with placing myself in the text, but questioning what role the life historians should play in the analysis and writing up. As I have suggested, it is in the final product, or text, that collaboration has proved the most difficult (Crapanzano

1980; Langness and Frank 1981; Visweswaran 1988). In attempting to construct a truly feminist, collaborative text, I conceived of three essential elements: my own self-reflexive account of the story; the intersubjective creation
of the story; and the actual stories of the life historians. How to present these
in a manner that did justice to each, while not reducing to a secondary position the story of the participants themselves, presents a continuing dilemma.
How do I balance the stories of the life historians, my reflexive account, and
their recollections of the research process without relegating their stories to a
lesser position?

Susan Geiger (1990:175) suggests that at one end of the spectrum of textual representation lies erasure of the participant through anonymous gen-
eralizations from her story that objectify her as just another 'text'. At the
other end lies total identification or attempted merger in an attempt to erase
not the person herself but the reality of differences. In order to avoid either
of these extremes, I hoped to represent the voices of the life historians in the
text by incorporating their feedback on the transcripts, engage them in a discussion of the salient themes and ultimately have them comment on the final
narrative and include their reactions to it in a written form.

At this point, the reaction of the life historians to my including them in the
interpretive process has been their acknowledgement that it is a subjective
process, and therefore their own interpretations are no more valid than
mine. Bonnie commented at our last session, after discussing what I felt were
the emergent themes, that she saw parallels between the research process
and the classroom. Just as she expected students to create their own meaning and take what they needed from the classroom experience, she trusted
that I would do the same.

In being left alone to the task of constructing their life histories, I am
acutely aware of not wanting to succumb to 'vanity ethnography' (Van
Maanen 1988). I am also self-conscious about experimenting with the text in
a way that might seem disrespectful or alienate the participants. I wonder, for
example, how they would feel if I presented them with an integrated text that
interwove the multiple voices throughout the text. Would they see this as
diminishing their story? If I used innovative postmodern textual representations, such as cartoons, poems, or pictures interspersed throughout the text
as a means of representing the complexity of our stories would they find this
a fair representation of their lives? In choosing to represent these narratives
in alternative forms, am I elevating my need to make a political and theoretical statement or am I trying to do justice to the stories of women teachers?

No conclusion

The dilemmas discussed here present no easy resolutions, if, in fact, there
are solutions at all. The questions of representation, self-reflexivity and

subjectivity in the collaborative process are ongoing. Will degree of reflexivity or subjectivity, or mode of representation provide 'better' criteria for establishing 'truth'? What about the goal of feminist research to be emancipatory or empowering? What criteria will be established to assess this? Again, I believe we are posing the wrong questions if we seek only to replace one form of measurement with another, for we are still trapped within an essentialist notion of truth.

My quest for understanding the collaborative process has not led me to new definitions or methods for establishing truth, be it partial, absolute, multiple or situated. It has led me to a deeper understanding of ways of knowing and how these are deeply embedded in the relational acts of the research process. My understanding of the multiple ways we create, negotiate and make sense of the power relationships in our lives has been enlarged. I only hope that my feminist position continues to situate me in, and alert me to, these crucial issues. For it is only from this position that I can even attempt to achieve the collaboration that I seek.

References

Abu-Lughod, L. (1990) The romance of resistance: Tracing transformations of power through Bedouin women. *American Ethnologist*, 17(1): 41–55.

Achebe, C. (1959) *Things Fall Apart*. New York: Fawcett Crest.

Adams, N. (1994) *'A Proper Little Lady' and Other Twisted Tales of Adolescent Femininity*. Doctoral dissertation, Department of Curriculum and Instruction, Louisiana State University, Baton Rouge, LA.

Adorno, T. (1973) *Negative Dialectics*. London: Routledge.

Agar, M.H. (1980) *The Professional Stranger: An Informal Introduction to Ethnography*. New York: Academic Press.

Aisenberg, N. and Harrison, M. (1988) *Women of Academe: Outsiders in the Sacred Grove*. Amherst, Mass.: University of Massachusetts Press.

Alcoff, L. (1989) Cultural feminism versus poststructuralism: The identity crisis in feminist theory, in M.R. Malson, J.F. O'Barr, S. Westphal-Wihl and M. Wyer (eds) *Feminist Theory in Practice and Process*. Chicago: University of Chicago Press.

Alcott, L.M. (1873) *Work: A Story of Experience*. Boston: Roberts Brothers.

Alpern, S., Antler, J., Perry, E. and Scobie, I. (1992) *The Challenge of Feminist Biography: Writing the Lives of Modern American Women*. Urbana, Ill: University of Illinois Press.

Althusser, L. (1971) *Lenin and Philosophy and Other Essays*. New York: Monthly Review Press.

Altieri, C. (1994) Intentionality without interiority: Wittgenstein and the dynamics of subjective agency, in C. McDonald and G. Wihl (eds) *Transformations in Personhood and Culture after Theory*. University Park, Penn.: The Pennsylvania State University Press.

Anderson, G. (1989) Critical ethnography in education: Origins, current status and new directions. *Review of Educational Research*, 59(3): 249–70.

Anderson, K., Armitage, S., Jack, D. and Wittner, J. (1990) Beginning where we are: Feminist methodology in oral history, in J. Nielson (ed.) *Feminist Research Methods*. Boulder, Colo.: Westview Press.

Anyon, J. (1983) Intersections of gender and class: Accommodation and resistance by working class and affluent females to contradictory sex-role ideologies, in S. Walker and L. Barton (eds) *Gender, Class and Education*. Sussex: Falmer Press.

Anzaldua, G. (1990) *Making Face, Making Soul.* San Francisco, Calif.: Aunt Lute Foundation Books.

Apple, M. (1978) The new sociology of education: Analyzing cultural and economic reproduction. *Harvard Educational Review,* 48(1): 495–503.

Apple, M. (1979) *Ideology and Curriculum.* London: Routledge & Kegan Paul.

Apple, M. (1983) Work, gender and teaching. *Teacher's College Record,* 84(3): 611–28.

Apple, M. (1985) Teaching and 'women's work': A comparative historical and ideological analysis. *Journal of Education,* 86(3): 455–73.

Aptheker, B. (1989) *Tapestries of Life.* Amherst, Mass.: University of Massachusetts Press.

Arnot, M. (1993) A crisis in patriarchy? British feminist educational politics and state regulation of gender, in M. Arnot and K. Weiler (eds) *Feminism and Social Justice in Education.* London: Falmer Press.

Ashton-Warner, S. (1963) *Teacher.* New York: Simon & Schuster.

Ayers, W. (1989) *The Good Preschool Teacher: Six Teachers Reflect on their Lives.* New York: Teachers College Press.

Bakhtin, M. (1981) *The Dialogic Imagination.* Austin, Tex.: University of Texas Press.

Bartky, S. (1990) *Femininity and Domination: Studies in the Phenomenology of Oppression.* New York: Routledge.

Bateson, M.C. (1989) *Composing a Life.* New York: Atlantic Monthly Press.

Beatty, B. (1990) 'A vocation from high': Kindergartening as an occupation for American women, in J. Antler and S.K. Biklen (eds) *Changing Education: Women as Radicals and Conservators.* Albany, N.Y.: State University of New York Press.

Belenky, M.F, Clinchy, B.M., Goldberger, N.R. and Tarule, J.M. (1986) *Women's Ways of Knowing.* New York: Basic Books.

Bell, S.G. and Yalom, M. (1990) *Revealing Lives: Autobiography, Biography and Gender.* Albany, N.Y.: State University of New York Press.

Benhabib, S. (1995) Feminism and postmodernism: An uneasy alliance, in S. Benhabib, J. Butler, D. Cornell and N. Fraser *Feminist Contentions: A Philosophical Exchange.* New York: Routledge Press.

Bernstein, B. (1975) *Class, Codes and Control: Towards a Theory of Educational Transmissions.* London: Routledge & Kegan Paul.

Best, S. and Kellner, D. (1991) *Postmodern Theory.* New York: The Guilford Press.

Biklen, S. (1983) Women in American elementary school teaching, in P. Schmuck (ed.) *Women Educators.* Albany, N.Y.: State University of New York Press.

Biklen, S. (1995) *School Work.* New York: Teachers College Press.

Bloom, A. (1987) *The Closing of the American Mind.* New York: Simon & Schuster.

Bloom, L. (1996) Stories of one's own: Nonunitary subjectivity in narrative representation. *Qualitative Inquiry,* 2(2): 176–97.

Bloom, L. (in press) *Under the Sign of Hope: Feminist Methodology and Narrative Interpretation.* Albany, N.Y.: State University of New York Press.

Bloom, L. and Munro, P. (1995) Conflicts of selves: Non-unitary subjectivity in women administrators' life history narratives, in A. Hatch and R. Wisniewski (eds) *Life history and narrative.* London: Falmer Press.

Bordo, S. (1993) Feminism, Foucault and the politics of the body, in C. Ramazanoglu (ed.) *Up Against Foucault.* New York: Routledge.

Bourdieu, P. (1977) *Outline of a Theory of Practice*. New York: Cambridge University Press.

Bowen, E.S. (1964) *Return to Laughter*. New York: Doubleday.

Bowers, C. and Flinders, D. (1990) *Responsive Teaching*. New York: Teachers College Press.

Bowles, S. and Gintis, H. (1976) *Schooling in Capitalist America*. New York: Basic Books.

Braidotti, R. (1994) Theories of gender, in C. McDonald and G. Wihl (eds) *Transformations in Personhood and Culture after Theory: The Languages of History, Aesthetics, and Ethics*. University Park, Penn.: Pennsylvania State University Press.

Britzman, D. (1991) *Practice Makes Practice*. Albany, N.Y.: State University of New York Press.

Britzman, D. (1995) Is there a queer theory? Or, stop thinking straight. *Educational Theory*, 45(2): 151–65.

Brodkey, L. and Fine, M. (1991) Presence of mind in the absence of body, in H. Giroux (ed.) *Postmodernism, Feminism and Cultural Politics*. Albany, N.Y.: State University of New York Press.

Bullough, R.V. (1990) Personal history and teaching metaphors in pre-service teacher education. Paper presented at the American Educational Research Association, Boston, Mass., April.

Bullough, R.V., Gitlin, A. and Goldstein, S. (1984) Ideology, teacher role, and resistance. *Teachers College Record*, 86: 339–58.

Butler, J. (1990) *Gender Trouble: Feminism and the Subversion of Identity*. London: Routledge.

Cain, M. (1993) Foucault, feminism and feeling: What Foucault can and cannot contribute to feminist epistemology, in C. Ramazanoglu (ed.) *Up Against Foucault*. New York: Routledge.

Cantarow, E. (1980) *Moving the Mountain: Women Working for Social Change*. New York: The Feminist Press.

Carter, P. (1992) The social status of women teachers in the early twentieth century, in R. Altenbaugh (ed.) *The Teachers' Voice*. London: The Falmer Press.

Casey, K. (1993) *I Answer With My Life: Life Histories of Women Teachers Working for Social Change*. New York: Routledge.

Chevigny, B. (1984) Daughters writing: Toward a theory of women's biography, in C. Ascher, L. DeSalvo and S. Ruddick (eds) *Between Women*. Boston, Mass.: Beacon Press.

Christ, C. (1986) *Diving Deep and Surfacing: Women Writers on Spiritual Quest*. Boston, Mass.: Beacon Press.

Christian, B. (1988) The race for theory. *Feminist Studies*, 14(1): 67–9.

Christman, J. (1988) Working the field as female friend. *Anthropology and Education Quarterly*, 19(2): 70–85.

Cixous, H. (1976) The laugh of the Medusa. *Signs: Journal of Women in Culture and Society*, 1(4): 875–93.

Cixous, H. (1981) Castration or decapitation? *Signs: Journal of Women in Culture and Society*, 7(1): 41–55.

Clark, S. (1990) A woman's place and the rural school in the United States. *Genders*, 8: 77–90.

Clifford, G. (1989) Man/woman/teacher: Gender, family and career in American educational history, in D. Warren (ed.) *American Teachers: Histories of a Profession at Work*. New York: Macmillan.

Clifford, J. (1986) Introduction: Partial truths, in J. Clifford and G.E. Marcus (eds) *Writing Culture: The Poetics and Politics of Ethnography*. Berkeley, Calif.: University of California Press.

Clifford, J. and Marcus, G.E. (1986) *Writing Culture: The Poetics and Politics of Ethnography*. Berkeley, Calif.: University of California Press.

Cocks, J. (1989) *The Oppositional Imagination: Feminism, Critique and Political Theory*. New York: Routledge.

Collins, P.H. (1990) *Black Feminist Thought: Knowledge, Consciousness and the Politics of Empowerment*. New York: Routledge.

Comstock, D. (1982) A method for critical research, in E. Bredo and W. Feinberg (eds) *Knowledge and Values in Social and Educational Research*. Philadelphia, Penn.: Temple University Press.

Connell, R.W., Ashedon, D., Kessler, S. and Dowsett, G. (1982) *Making the Difference: Schools, Families and Social Division*. North Sydney, Aus.: George Allen & Unwin.

Connelly, F.M. and Clandinin, D.J. (1988) *Teachers as Curriculum Planners: Narratives of Experience*. New York: Teachers College Press.

Connelly, F.M. and Clandinin, D.J. (1990) Stories of experience and narrative inquiry. *Educational Researcher*, 19(4): 2–14.

Conway, J. (1971) Women reformers and American culture, 1870–1930. *Journal of Social History*, 5(2): 164–77.

Cook, B. (1977) Female support networks and political activism: Lilian Wald, Crystal Eastman, Emma Goldman. *Chrysalis*, 3: 43–61.

Cott, N. (1977) *The Bonds of Womanhood: 'Women's sphere' in New England, 1780–1835*. New Haven, Conn.: Yale University Press.

Crapanzano, V. (1980) *Tuhami: Portrait of a Moroccan*. Chicago. Ill.: University of Chicago Press.

Cuban, L. (1984) *How Teachers Taught*. New York: Longman.

Cubberly, E. (1914) *Rural Life and Education: A Study of the Rural-School Problem as a Phase of the Rural-Life Problem*. Boston, Mass.: Houghton Mifflin.

Cuffaro, H. K. (1991) A view of materials as the texts of the early childhood curriculum, in B. Spodek and O. Saracho (eds) *Issues in Early Childhood Education*. New York: Teachers College Press.

Daly, M. (1973) *Beyond God the Father: Towards a Philosophy of Women's Liberation*. Boston, Mass.: Beacon Press.

Davis, K. and Fisher, S. (1993) Power and the female subject, in S. Fisher and K. Davis (eds) *Negotiating the Margins: The Gendered Discourses of Power and Resistance*. New Brunswick, N.J.: Rutgers University Press.

de Beauvoir, S. (1953) *The Second Sex*, tr. H.M. Parshly. New York: Bantam Books.

de Lauretis, T. (1987) *Technologies of Gender: Essays on Theory, Film and Fiction*. Bloomington, Ind.: Indiana University Press.

Denzin, N. (1970) *The Research Act in Sociology: A Theoretical Introduction to Sociological Methods*. Chicago: Aldine.

Denzin, N. and Lincoln, I. (eds) (1994) *Handbook of Qualitative Research*. London: Sage.

Doll, W. (1993) *A Post-modern Perspective on Curriculum*. New York: Teachers College Press.

Dollard, J. (1935) *Criteria for the Life History*. New York: Libraries Press.

Donovan, F.R. (1938) *The School Ma'am*. New York: Frederick A. Stokes.

Duelli-Klein, R. (1983) How to do what we want to do: Thoughts about feminist methodology, in G. Bowles and R. Duelli-Klein (eds) *Theories of Women's Studies*. London: Routledge.

Ellsworth, E. (1989) Why doesn't this feel empowering? Working through the repressive myths of critical pedagogy. *Harvard Educational Review*, 59(3): 297–324.

Etter-Lewis, G. (1993) *My Soul is My Own: Oral Narratives of African American Women in the Professions*. New York: Routledge.

Everhart, R. (1977) Between stranger and friend: Some consequences of 'long term' field work in schools. *American Educational Research Journal*, 14: 1–15.

Fanon, F. (1961) *The Wretched of the Earth*, tr. C. Farrington. New York: Grove Press.

Feinberg, W. (1993) *Japan and the Pursuit of a New American Identity: Work and Education in a Multicultural Age*. New York: Routledge.

Feldman, A. (1991) *Formations of Violence: The Narrative of the Body and Political Terror in Northern Ireland*. Chicago, Ill.: University of Chicago Press.

Fine, L.M. (1990) *The Souls of the Skyscraper: Female Clerical Workers in Chicago, 1870–1930*. Philadelphia, Penn.: Temple University Press.

Flax, J. (1989) Postmodernism and gender relations in feminist theory, in M.R. Malson, J.F. O'Barr, S. Westphal-Wihl and M. Wyer (eds) *Feminist Theory in Practice and Process*. Chicago, Ill.: University of Chicago Press.

Flax, J. (1990) *Thinking Fragments: Psychoanalysis, Feminism and Postmodernism in the Contemporary West*. Berkeley, Calif.: University of California Press.

Foucault, M. (1978) *The History of Sexuality. Vol 1: An Introduction*. New York: Random House.

Foucault, M. (1979) *Discipline and Punish: The Birth of Prison*. New York: Vintage Books.

Foucault, M. (1980) *Power Knowledge: Selected Interviews and Other Writings, 1972–1977*. Sussex: Harvester Press.

Foucault, M. (1984) Excerpts from *Discipline and Punish* (tr. A. Sheridan), in P. Rabinow (ed.) *The Foucault Reader*. New York: Pantheon Books.

Fraser, N. (1989) *Unruly Practices: Power, Discourse and Gender in Contemporary Social Theory*. Minneapolis, Minn.: University of Minnesota Press.

Fraser, N. and Nicholson, L.J. (1990) Social criticism without philosophy: An encounter between feminism and postmodernism, in L. Nicholson (ed.) *Feminism/Postmodernism*. New York: Routledge.

Freeman, M. (1993) *Rewriting the Self: History, Memory, Narrative*. New York: Routledge.

Freire, P. (1973) *Pedagogy of the Oppressed*. New York: Seabury Press.

Friedan, B. (1974) *The Feminine Mystique*, 2nd edn. New York: Dell.

Geertz, C. (1973) *The Interpretation of Cultures*. New York: Basic Books.

Geiger, S. (1986) Women's life histories: Methods and content. *Signs: Journal of Women in Culture and Society*, 11(2): 334–51.

Geiger, S. (1990) What's so feminist about women's oral history? *Journal of Women's History*, 2(1): 169–82.

Gilbert, S. and Gubar, S. (1979) *The Madwoman in the Attic: The Woman Writer and the Nineteenth-century Literary Imagination*. New Haven, Conn.: Yale University Press.

Gilligan, C., Lyons, N.P. and Hamner, T.J. (eds) (1990) *Making Connections: The Relational World of Adolescent Girls at Emma Willard School*. Cambridge, Mass.: Harvard University Press.

Gilman, C.P. (1979) *Herland*, with an introduction by Ann J. Lane. London: Women's Press.

Gilman, C.P. (1981) *The Charlotte Perkins Gilman Reader: The Yellow and Other Fiction*, edited and introduced by Ann J. Lane. London: Women's Press.

Gilmore, L. (1994) *Autobiographics: A Feminist Theory of Women's Self-Representation*. Ithaca, N.Y.: Cornell University Press.

Giroux, H.A. (1983) *Theory and Resistance in Education*. South Hadley, Mass.: Bergin & Garvey.

Giroux, H.A. (1986) Curriculum, teaching and the resisting intellectual. *Curriculum and Teaching*, 1(1/2): 33–42.

Giroux, H.A. (1988) *Teachers as Intellectuals*. South Hadley, Mass.: Bergin & Garvey.

Gitlin, A.D. (1990) Educative research, voice and school change. *Harvard Educational Review*, 60(4): 443–66.

Golde, P. (1970) *Women in the Field: Anthropological Experiences*. Chicago: Aldine.

Goodson, I. (1988) *The Making of the Curriculum*. New York: Falmer Press.

Goodson, I. (ed.) (1992) *Studying Teachers' Lives*. New York: Teachers College Press.

Goodson, I. (1995) The story so far: Personal knowledge and the political, in J.A. Hatch and R. Wisniewski (eds) *Life History and Narrative*. London: Falmer Press.

Goodson, I. and Cole, A. (1994) Exploring the teacher's professional knowledge, in D. McLaughlin and W.G. Tierney (eds) *Naming Silenced Lives*. New York: Routledge.

Gordon, L.D. (1990) *Gender and Higher Education in the Progressive Era*. New Haven, Conn.: Yale University Press.

Gore, J. (1993) *The Struggle for Pedagogies*. New York: Routledge.

Gough, N. (1994) Narration, reflection, diffraction: Aspects of fiction in educational inquiry. *Australian Educational Researcher*, 21(3): 1–23.

Gramsci, A. (1971) *Selections From the Prison Notebooks*. New York: International.

Greene, M. (1975) Curriculum and cultural transformation: A humanistic view. *Cross Currents*, 25(2): 175–86.

Greene, M. (1992) There's no identity like no identity: Poststructuralist perspectives. Paper presented at the American Educational Research Association, San Francisco, Calif., April.

Grimshaw, J. (1993) Practices of freedom, in C. Ramazanoglu (ed.) *Up Against Foucault*. New York: Routledge.

Grumet, M. (1988) *Bitter Milk: Women and Teaching*. Amherst, Mass.: University of Massachusetts Press.

Grumet, M. (1990) On daffodils that come before the swallow dares, in E.W. Eisner and A. Peshkin (eds) *Qualitative Inquiry in Education: The Continuing Debate*. New York: Teachers College Press.

Grumet, M. (1991) The politics of personal knowledge, in C. Witherell and N. Noddings (eds) *Stories Lives Tell*. New York: Teachers College Press.

Habermas, J. (1976) *Communication and the Evolution of Society*. Boston, Mass.: Beacon Press.

Hancock, E. (1989) *The Girl Within*. New York: Fawcett Columbine.

Harding, S. (1987) Introduction: Is there a feminist method?, in S. Harding (ed.) *Feminism and Methodology*. Bloomington, Ind.: Indiana University Press.

Harding, S. (1989) Is there a feminist method?, in N. Tuana (ed.) *Feminism and Science*. Bloomington, Ind.: Indiana University Press.

Harrison, E. (1890) *A Study of Child-nature*. Chicago, Ill.: The Lakeside Press.

Hartstock, N. (1990) Foucault on power: A theory for women?, in L. Nicholson (ed.) *Feminism/Postmodernism*. New York: Routledge.

Haug, F. (1987) *Female Sexualization: A Collective Work of Memory*. London: Verso.

Hawkesworth, M. (1989) Knowers, knowing, known: Feminist theory and claims of truth, in M.R. Malson, J.F. O'Barr, S. Westphal-Wihl and M. Wyer (eds) *Feminist Theory into Practice and Process*. Chicago, Ill.: University of Chicago Press.

Heilbrun, C. (1988) *Writing a Woman's Life*. New York: W.W. Norton.

Hekman, S. (1990) *Gender and Knowledge: Elements of a Postmodern Feminism*. Boston, Mass.: Northeastern University Press.

Hekman, S. (1995) Subjects and agents: The question for feminism, in J. Gardiner (ed.) *Provoking Agents: Gender and Agency in Theory and Practice*. Urbana, Ill.: University of Illinois Press.

Henriques, J., Hollway, W., Urwin, C., Venn, C. and Walkerdine, V. (1984) *Changing the Subject: Psychology, Social Regulation and Subjectivity*. London: Methuen.

Hirsch, E.D. (1988) *Cultural Literacy: What Every American Needs to Know*. New York: Random House.

Hoffman, N. (1981) *Women's True Profession: Voices for the History of Teaching*. New York: McGraw-Hill.

hooks, b. (1989) *Talking Back: Thinking Feminist, Thinking Black*. Boston, Mass.: South End Press.

hooks, b. (1990) *Yearning: Race, Gender and Cultural Politics*. Boston, Mass.: South End Press.

Hudson, B. (1984) Femininity and adolescence, in A. McRobbie and M. Nava (eds) *Gender and Generation*. London: Macmillan.

Hurston, Z.N. (1969) *Mules and Men*, with an introduction by Fraz Boas. New York: Negro Universities Press.

Irigaray, L. (1985) *Speculum of the Other Woman*, tr. G. Gill. Paris: Editions de Minuit.

Jackson, P. (1968) *Life in Classrooms*. New York: Holt, Rinehart and Winston.

Jacobs, M. (1992) Personal communication.

Jacobs, M., Munro, P. and Adams, N. (1995) Palimpsest: (Re)reading women's lives. *Qualitative Inquiry*, 1: 327–45.

Jagla, V.M. (1992) Teachers everyday imagination and intuition, in W. Schubert and W. Ayers (eds) *Teacher Lore*. New York: Longman.

Jipson, J., Munro, P., Victor, S., Froude Jones, K. and Freed-Rowland, G. (1995) *Repositioning Feminism and Education: Perspectives on Educating for Social Change*. Westport, Conn.: Bergin & Garvey.

Jones, A. (1993) Becoming a 'girl': Post-structuralist suggestions for educational research. *Gender and Education*, 5(2): 157–66.

Kaplan, E.A. (1993) Madonna politics: Perversion, repression, or subversion? Or masks and/as master-y, in C. Schwichtenberg (ed.) *The Madonna Connection*. Boulder, Colo.: Westview Press.

Kaplan, E.A. (1994) *French Lessons: A Memoir*. Chicago, Ill.: University of Chicago Press.

Kaufman, P. (1984) *Women Teachers on the Frontier*. New Haven, Conn.: Yale University Press.

Keller, E.F. (1985) *Reflections on Gender and Science*. New Haven, Conn.: Yale University Press.

Khayatt, M. (1992) *Lesbian Teachers*. New York: State University of New York Press.

Kliebard, H. (1986) *The Struggle for the American Curriculum, 1893–1958*. Boston, Mass.: Routledge & Kegan Paul.

Knowles, G.J. and Ems, D. (1990) The convergence of teachers, educators, and pre-service teachers' personal histories: Shaping pedagogy. Paper presented at the American Educational Research Association, Boston, Mass., April.

Kohli, W. (1996) Risky business: The new 'R&D' (risky and dangerous) in teacher education, presented at the symposium Rethinking the lives of women educators: Poststructuralist and materialist feminist approaches, American Educational Research Conference, New York, April.

Langness, L.L. and Frank, G. (1981) *Lives: An Anthropologial Approach to Biography*. Novato, Calif.: Chandler & Sharp.

Larabee, D.F. (1992) Power, knowledge and the rationalization of teaching: A genealogy of the movement to professionalize teaching. *Harvard Educational Review*, 62(2): 123–54.

Lather, P. (1986) Research as praxis. *Harvard Educational Review*, 56(3): 257–77.

Lather, P. (1991) *Getting Smart: Feminist Research and Pedagogy Within the Postmodern*. New York: Routledge.

Leck, G. (1987) Feminist pedagogy, liberation theory and the traditional schooling paradigm. *Educational Theory*, 37(30): 343–54.

LeCompte, M. (1994) A framework for hearing silence: What does telling stories mean when we are supposed to be doing science?, in D. McLaughlin and W.G. Tierney (eds) *Naming Silenced Lives*. New York: Routledge.

Lesko, N. (1988) *Symbolizing Society*. Basingstoke: Falmer Press.

Lieberman, A. (1988) *Building a Professional Culture in School*. New York: Teachers College Press.

Lincoln, I. (1994) I and thou: Method, voice and roles in research with the silenced, in D. McLaughlin and W.G. Tierney (eds) *Naming Silenced Lives*. New York: Routledge.

Lorde, A. (1984) *Sister Outsider*. Trumansburgh, N.Y.: Crossing Press.

Lortie, D. (1975) *School Teacher*. Chicago, Ill.: University of Chicago Press.

Luke, C. and Gore, J. (1992) *Feminisms and Critical Pedagogy*. New York: Routledge.

McLaren, P. (1994) Border disputes: Multicultural narrative, identity formation, and critical pedagogy in postmodern America, in D. McLaughlin and W.G. Tierney (eds) *Naming Silenced Lives*. New York: Routledge.

McLaren, P. (1989) *Life in Schools*. New York: Longman.

Mackethan, L.H. (1990) *Daughters of Time*. Athens: University of Georgia Press.

McLaughlin, D. and Tierney, W.G. (1993) *Naming Silenced Lives*. New York: Routledge.

McRobbie, A. (1982) The politics of feminist research: Between text, talk and action. *Feminist Review*, 12: 46–57.

McWilliams, E. (1994) *In Broken Images: Feminist Tales for a Different Teacher Education*. New York: Teachers College Press.

Mahoney, M. and Yngnesson, B. (1992) The constitution of subjectivity and the paradox of resistance: Reintegrating feminist anthropology and psychology. *Signs: Journal of Women in Culture and Society*, 18(11): 44–73.

Makler, A. (1991) Imagining history. A good and well-formed argument, in C. Witherell and N. Noddings (eds) *Stories Lives Tell*. New York: Teachers College Press.

Mandelbaum, D.G. (1973) The study of life history: Gandhi. *Current Anthropology*, 14(3): 177–206.

Marcus, J. (1984) Invisible mending, in C. Ascher, L. DeSalvo and S. Ruddick (eds) *Between Women*. Boston, Mass.: Beacon Press.

Marcus, G.E. and Fischer, M. (1986) *Anthropology as Cultural Critique*. Chicago, Ill.: University of Chicago Press.

Marshall, J.D. (1995) Putting the political back into autonomy, in W. Kohli (ed.) *Critical Conversations in Philosophy of Education*. New York: Routledge.

Martin, J.R. (1994) Methodological essentialism, false difference, and other dangerous traps. *Signs*, 19(3): 630–57.

Martusewicz, R.A. (1992) Mapping the terrain of the postmodern subject, in W. Pinar and W. Reynolds (eds) *Understanding Curriculum as Phenomenological and Deconstructed Text*. New York: Teachers College Press.

Mascia-Lees, F.E., Sharpe, P. and Cohen, C. (1989) The post-modern turn in anthropology: Cautions from a feminist perspective. *Signs: Journal of Women in Culture and Society*, 15(1): 7–34.

Mbilinyi, M. (1989) I'd have been a man, in Personal Narratives Group (eds) *Interpreting Women's Lives*. Bloomington, Ind.: Indiana University Press.

Meyer, A.L. (1989) Agnes Louise Adams. *Childhood Education*, 65(4): 228–9.

Meyerowitz, J.J. (1988) *Women Adrift: Independent Wage Earners in Chicago, 1880–1930*. Chicago, Ill.: University of Chicago Press.

Middleton, S. (1993) *Educating Feminists: Life Histories and Pedagogy*. New York: Teachers College Press.

Mies, M. (1983) Towards a methodology for feminist research, in G. Bowles and R. Duelli-Klein (eds) *Theories of Women's Studies*. London: Routledge.

Miller, J. (1989) *Creating Spaces, Finding Voices*. New York: State University of New York Press.

Miller, N. (1989) Changing the subject, in E. Weed (ed.) *Coming to Terms: Feminism, Theory, Politics*. New York: Routledge.

Miller, N. (1991) *Getting Personal: Feminist Occasions and Other Autobiographical Acts*. New York: Routledge.

Millet, K. (1970) *Sexual Politics*. New York: Doubleday.

Minh-ha, T. (1987) Difference: 'A special third world women issue'. *Feminist Review*, 25: 5–22.

Minh-ha, T. (1991) *When the Moon Waxes Red*. New York: Routledge.

Moi, T. (1985) *Sexual/textual Politics: Feminist Literary Theory*. New York: Methuen.

Morrison, T. (1992) Friday on the Potomac, in T. Morrison (ed.) *Race-ing Justice, En-gendering Power*. New York: Pantheon Books.

Munro, P. (1993) Continuing dilemmas of life history research: A reflexive account of feminist qualitative research, in D. Flinders and G. Mills (eds) *Theory and Concepts in Qualitative Research: Perspectives From the Field*. New York: Teachers College Press.

Munro, P. (1995) Women educators as activists: Expanding the definitions. *Social Education*, 59(5): 274–9.

Munro, P. (1996) Resisting 'Resistance': Stories women teachers tell. *Journal of Curriculum Theorizing*, 12(1): 16–28.

Munro, P. (1998) Engendering curriculum history, in W.F. Pinar (ed.) *Curriculum: Toward New Identities in/for the Field*. New York: Garland Press.

Munro, P. (in press) Turning facts into puzzles: Feminist and poststructuralist perspectives on the history of early childhood education, in M. Hauser and J. Jipson (eds) *Intersections: Feminisms/ Early Childhoods*. New York: Peter Lang.

Myerhoff, B. (1982) Life history among the elderly, in J.Ruby (ed.) *A Crack in the Mirror: Reflexive Perspectives in Anthropology*. Philadelphia, Penn.: University of Pennsylvania Press.

Narayan, U. (1988) Working together across difference: Some considerations on emotions and political practice. *Hypatia*, 3: 31–47.

National Commission of Excellence in Education (1983) *Nation at Risk*. Washington, D.C.: NCEE.

Nelson, L. (1993) Epistemological communities, in L. Alcoff and E. Potter (eds) *Feminist Epistemologies*. New York: Routledge.

Ngugi, J. (1964) *Weep Not, Child*. New York: Macmillan.

Nicholson, L. (1994) Interpreting gender. *Signs: Journal of Women in Culture and Society*, 20(1): 79–103.

Nietzsche, F. (1956) *The Birth of Tragedy and the Genealogy of Morals*. Garden City, N.Y.: Doubleday.

Oram, A. (1989) Embittered, sexless or homosexual: Attacks on spinster teachers 1918–1939, in A. Angerman, G. Bennema, A. Keunen, V. Pucls and J. Zirkzee (eds) *Current Issues in Women's History*. London: Routledge.

Orner, M. (1992) Interrupting the calls for student voice in 'liberatory' education: A feminist poststructuralist perspective, in C. Luke and J. Gore (eds) *Feminism and Critical Pedagogy*. New York: Routledge.

Pagano, J. (1990) *Exiles and Communities: Teaching in the Patriarchal Wilderness*. Albany, N.Y.: State University of New York Press.

Parker, S. C. and Temple, A. (1925) *Unified Kindergarten and First-grade Teaching*. Boston, Mass.: Ginn and Company.

Passerini, L. (1989) Women's personal narratives: Myths, experiences, and emotions, in Personal Narratives Group (eds) *Interpreting Women's Lives*. Bloomington, Ind.: Indiana University Press.

Paules, G. (1991) *Dishing it Out*. Philadelphia, Penn.: Temple University Press.

Pencier, I.B. (1967) *The History of the Laboratory Schools, the University of Chicago, 1896–1965*. Chicago, Ill.: Quadrangle Books.

Personal Narratives Group (1989) *Interpreting Women's Lives: Feminist Theory and Personal Narratives*. Bloomington, Ind.: Indiana University Press.

Peshkin, A. (1988) In search of subjectivity – one's own. *Educational Researcher*, 17(7): 17–21.

Pignatelli, F. (1993) What can I do? Foucault on freedom and the question of teacher agency. *Educational Theory*, 43(4): 411–32.

Pinar, W. (1975) *Curriculum Theorizing: The Reconceptualists*. Berkeley, Calif.: McCutcheon.

Pinar, W. (1983) Curriculum as gender text: Notes on reproduction, resistance and male–male relations. *Journal of Curriculum Theorizing*, 5(1): 26–52.

Pinar, W.F. (1994) *Autobiography, Sexuality and Curriculum Theory*. New York: Peter Lang.

Pinar, W.F. and Grumet, M.R. (1976) *Toward a Poor Curriculum*. Dubuque, Iowa: Kendall/Hunt.

Pinar, W.F., Reynolds, W.M., Slattery, P. and Taubman, P.M. (1995) *Understanding Curriculum: An Introduction to the Study of Historical and Contemporary Curriculum Discourses*. New York: Peter Lang.

Plummer, K. (1983) *Documents of Life: An Introduction to the Problems and Literature of a Humanistic Method*. London: Allen & Unwin.

Polkinghorne, D.E. (1988) *Narrative Knowing and the Human Sciences*. Albany, N.Y.: State University of New York Press.

Portelli, A. (1993) *The Death of Luigi Trastulli and Other Stories*. Albany, N.Y.: State University of New York Press.

Powdermaker, H. (1966) *Stranger and Friend: The Ways of an Anthropologist*. New York: Norton.

Prentice, A. and Theobold, M. (eds) (1991) *Women who Taught: Perspectives on the History of Women and Teaching*. Toronto: University of Toronto Press.

Quantz, R.A. (1985) The complex visions of female teachers and the failure of unionization in the 1930s. *History of Education Quarterly*, 25: 439–58.

Ravitch, D. (1974) *The Great School Wars: New York City, 1805–1973*. New York: Basic Books.

Reinharz, S. (1979) *On Becoming a Social Scientist: From Survey Research and Participant Observation to Experiential Analysis*. San Francisco, Calif.: Jossey-Bass.

Ricoeur, P. (1974) *The Conflict of Interpretations*. Evanston, Ill.: Northwestern University Press.

Riley, D. (1989) Feminism and the consolidation of 'women' in history, in E. Weed (ed.) *Coming to Terms*. New York: Routledge.

Riviere, J. (1985) Womanliness as masquerade, in V. Burgin, J. Donald and C. Kaplan (eds) *Formations of Fantasy*. London: Methuen.

Robertson, C. (1983) In pursuit of life histories: The problem of bias. *Frontiers*, 7(2): 63–9.

Roman, L. (1988) Intimacy, labor, and class: Ideologies of feminine sexuality in the punk slam dance, in L. Roman and L. Christian-Smith (eds) *Becoming Feminine: The Politics of Popular Culture*. Basingstoke: Falmer Press.

Roman, L. (1989). Double exposure: The politics of feminist materialist ethnography. Paper presented at the annual meeting of the American Educational Research Association, San Francisco, Calif., April.

Roman, L. and Apple, M.W. (1990) Is naturalism a move away from positivism?: Materialist and feminist approaches to subjectivity in ethnographic research, in E. W. Eisner and A. Peshkin (eds) *Qualitative Inquiry in Education: The Continuing Debate*. New York: Teachers College Press.

Ropers-Huilman, B. (1998) *Feminist Teaching in Theory and Practice: Situating Power and Knowledge in Poststructural Classrooms*. New York: Teachers College Press.

Rosenberg, R. (1982) *Beyond Separate Spheres: Intellectual Roots of Modern Feminism*. New Haven, Conn.: Yale University Press.

Rosenwald, G.C. and Ochenberg, R. L. (1992) Introduction: Life stories, cultural politics, and self-understanding, in G.C. Rosenwald and R.L. Ochenberg (eds) *Storied Lives*. New Haven, Conn.: Yale University Press.

Ruby, J. (ed.) (1982) *A Crack in the Mirror: Reflexive Perspectives in Anthropology*. Philadelphia, Penn.: University of Pennsylvania Press.

Ryan, M.P. (1979) *Womanhood in America: From Colonial Times to the Present*. New York: New Viewpoints.

Sawicki, J. (1991) *Disciplining Foucault: Feminism, Power and the Body*. New York: Routledge.

Scheurich, J.J. (1996) The masks of validity: a deconstructive investigation. *International Journal of Qualitative Studies in Education*, 9(1): 49–61.

Schubert, W.H. (1991) Teacher lore: A basis for understanding praxis, in C. Witherell and N. Noddings (eds) *Stories Lives Tell*. New York: Teachers College Press.

Schubert, W.H. and Ayers, W.C. (1992) *Teacher Lore: Learning From our Own Experiences*. New York: Longman.

Scott, A.F. (1993) *Natural Allies: Women's Associations in American History*. Urbana, Ill.: University of Illinois Press.

Scott, J.C. (1985) *Weapons of the Weak: Everyday Forms of Peasant Resistance*. New Haven, Conn.: Yale University Press.

Scott, J.C. (1989) Gender: A useful category of historical analysis, in E. Weed (ed.) *Coming to Terms*. New York: Routledge.

Sembene, O. (1962) *God's Bits of Wood*, tr. Francis Price. New York: Doubleday.

Sheridan, M. and Salaff, J.W. (1984) *Lives: Chinese Working Women*. Bloomington, Ind.: Indiana University Press.

Shostak, M. (1981) *Nisa*. New York: Vintage Books.

Showalter, E. (ed.) (1978) *These Modern Women: Autobiographical Essays from the Twenties*. Old Westbury, N.Y.: Feminist Press.

Sikes, P.J., Measor, L. and Woods, P. (1985) *Teacher Careers: Crises and Continuities*. London: Falmer Press.

Simon, R.I. (1983) But who will let you do it?: Counter-hegemonic possibilities for work education. *Journal of Education*, 165: 235–56.

Smith, D. (1987) *The Everyday World as Problematic*. Boston, Mass.: Northeastern University Press.

Smith, P. (1988) *Discerning the Subject*. Minneapolis, Minn.: University of Minnesota Press.

Smith, S. (1987) *A Poetic on Women's Autobiography: Marginality and the Fictions of Self-representation*. Bloomington, Ind.: Indiana University Press.

Smith, S. (1993a) *Subjectivity, Identity, and the Body*. Bloomington, Ind.: Indiana University Press.

Smith, S. (1993b) Who's talking/ Who's talking back? The subject of personal narrative. *Signs: Journal of Women in Culture and Society*, 18(2): 329–407.

Smith-Rosenberg, C (1985) *Disorderly Conduct: Visions of Gender in Victorian America*. New York: Alfred A. Knopf.

Smyth, J. (1991) Instructional supervision and the redefinition of who does it in schools. *Journal of Curriculum and Supervision*, 7(1): 90–9.

Snyder, A. (1972) *Dauntless Women in Childhood Education: 1856–1931*. Washington D.C.: Association for Childhood Education International.

Soper, K. (1993) Productive contradictions, in C. Ramazanoglu (ed.) *Up Against Foucault*. New York: Routledge.

Sparkes, A.C. (1994) Self, silence and invisibility as a beginning teacher: a life history of lesbian experience. *British Journal of Sociology of Education*, 15(1): 93–118.

Spelman, E. (1988) *Inessential Women*. Boston, Mass.: Beacon Press.

Spivak, G. (1987) *In Other Worlds: Essays in Cultural Politics*. New York: Methuen.

Stacey, J. (1988) Can there be feminist ethnography? *Women's Studies International Forum*, 11(1): 21–7.

Stanley, W. (1992) *Curriculum for Utopia*. Albany, N.Y.: State University of New York Press.

Steedman, C. (1990) *Childhood, Culture and Class in Britain: Margaret McMillan, 1860–1931*. New Brunswick, N.J.: Rutgers University Press.

Stewart, A. (1994) Toward a feminist strategy for studying women's lives, in C. Franz and A. Stewart (eds)*Women Creating Lives*. Boulder, Colo.: Westview Press.

Strathern, M. (1987) An awkward relationship: The case of feminism and anthropology. *Signs: Journal of Women in Culture and Society*, 12(2): 276–92.

Tyack, D. (1974) *The One Best System*. Cambridge, Mass.: Harvard University Press.

Urban, W. (1982) *Why Teachers Organized*. Detroit, Mich.: Wayne State University Press.

Urban, W. (1989) Teacher activism, in D. Warren (ed.) *American Teachers: A Profession at Work*. New York: Macmillan.

Van Maanen, J. (1988) *Tales of the Field*. Chicago, Ill.: University of Chicago Press.

Visweswaran, K. (1988) Defining feminist ethnography, *Inscriptions*, (3/4): 27–44.

Walkerdine, V. (1990) *Schoolgirl Fictions*. London: Verso.

Watson, L. and Watson-Franke, F. (1985) *Interpreting Life Histories: An Anthropological Inquiry*. New Brunswick, N.J.: Rutgers University Press.

Weber, E. (1969) *The Kindergarten: Its Encounter with Educational Thought in America*. New York: Teachers College Press.

Weiler, K. (1988) *Women Teaching for Social Change*. South Hadley, Mass.: Bergin & Garvey.

Weiler, K. (1991) Freire and a feminist pedagogy of difference. *Harvard Educational Review*, 61(4): 449–74.

Weiler, K. (1993) Feminism and the struggle for a democratic education: A view from the United States, in M. Arnot and K. Weiler (eds) *Feminism and Social Justice in Education*. London: Falmer Press.

Weiler, K. (1994) The lives of teachers: Feminism and life history narratives. *Educational Researcher*, 23(4): 30–3.

Weiler, K. (in press) Teaching in the California countryside 1850–1950. Berkeley, Calif.: University of California Press.

Westbrook, R.B. (1991) *John Dewey and American Democracy*. Ithaca, N.Y.: Cornell University Press.

Westphal, S. (1994) Stories of gender, in C. McDonald and G. Wihl (eds) *Transformations in Personhood and Culture after Theory: The Languages of History, Aesthetics, and Ethics*. University Park, Penn.: Pennsylvania State University Press.

Wexler, P. (1976) *The Sociology of Education: Beyond Equality*. Indianapolis, Ind.: Bobbs-Merrill.

Wexler, P. (1987) *Social Analysis of Education*. New York: Routledge & Kegan Paul.

Whitson, T. (1991) Poststructuralist pedagogy as counter-hegemonic praxis (can we find the baby in the bathwater?). *Education and Society*, 9(1): 73–86.

Williams, R. (1977) *Marxism and Literature*. Oxford: Oxford University Press.

Willis, P. (1977) *Learning to Labour: How Working Class Kids get Working Class Jobs*. Westmead: Saxon House.

Witherell, C. and Noddings, N. (1991) *Stories Lives Tell*. New York: Teachers College Press.

Wittig, M. (1983) The point of view: Universal or particular? *Feminist Issues*, 3(2): 63–9.

Wolcott, H. (1990) On seeking – and rejecting – validity in qualitative research, in E. Eisner and A. Peshkin (eds) *Qualitative Inquiry in Education: The Continuing Debate*. New York: Teachers College Press.

Wrigley, J. (1982) *Class Politics and Public School: Chicago 1900–1950*. New Brunswick, N.J.: Rutgers University Press.

Yates, L. (1993) Feminism and Australian state policy: Some questions from the 1990s, in M. Arnot and K. Weiler (eds) *Feminism and Social Justice in Education*. London: Falmer Press.

Young, R. (1990) *White Mythologies: Writing History and the West*. New York: Routledge.

Zinn, H. (1980) *A People's History of the United States*. New York: Harper & Row.

Index

Note: Page numbers followed by *n* refer to notes